# INTERPRETATIO RERUM

Archaeological Essays on Objects and Meaning

D1727803

# ARCHAEOLOGIA TRANSATLANTICA XVII

A Series in Mediterranean Archaeology

founded by

Tony Hackens +
Doyen de la Faculté de philosophie et lettres
Université Catholique de Louvain, Louvain-la-Neuve

R. Ross Holloway
Professor of Central Mediterranean Archaeology
and Director of the Center for Old World Archaeology and Art
Brown University, Providence

# INTERPRETATIO RERUM

Archaeologia Transatlantica
XVII

Archaeological Essays on Objects and Meaning
by Students of R. Ross Holloway

edited by

Susan S. Lukesh

CENTER FOR OLD WORLD ARCHAEOLOGY AND ART
BROWN UNIVERSITY
PROVIDENCE, RHODE ISLAND

1999

# Contents

# PREFACE

R. Ross Holloway was honored with the Archaeological Institute of America Gold Medal at the annual meetings in 1995. A year later at the subsequent A.I.A. Annual Meetings, a colloquium in his honor – as recipient of the Gold Medal – offered a series of papers delivered by his former students and colleagues: Image and Medium in Ancient Art and Coinage. Shortly after the 1996 conference and the very successful panel of papers, I e-mailed Tony Hackens, Dean of the Faculty of Philosophy and Letters, Catholic University of Louvain, Louvain-la-Neuve, long term close friend and colleague of Ross to inquire of the possibility of his publishing these papers. I received an immediate and enthusiastic response, as I expected I would: Tony saw it as a wonderful opportunity to produce a Festschrift for someone with whom he had shared, planned and produced a great deal since they met in the early 1960's. Of all of Ross's students I perhaps had the most direct and closest relationship with Tony, since I had begun working with him in 1975 when I had the pleasure of serving as Associate Curator of Antiquities at the Rhode Island School of Design Museum of Art during the publication of his volume on the classical jewelry in their collection.[1] Those of you fortunate enough to know Tony will recognize his voice (and his unrealistic expectations of timing) even in his e-mail response, and so I quote from it, unstructured as e-mail often tends to be:

> The answer is yes… As you know we voted a honorary degree to your mentor and master: he will receive it ceremoniously on the 26th of April… The whole volume should hold 160 pages? Deadline end of June, so we can read it in Corfu and prepare there… I have a Bios kai Erga of Ross. And I can write some friendly words…photographs welcome: in the digs and in toga, old photos from Princeton or

Rome?… What symbolic word for his oeuvre and personality? To be thought over in between us.

> With many friendly thoughts.

> Yours as ever

> Tony Hackens

Ten months after this response, Tony died suddenly at the age of 56, and our plans for this volume naturally took a back seat to our sorrow as well as the necessity of completing the many projects that Tony already had in production. Last summer Ross suggested that Archaeologica Transatlantica, his joint creation with Tony in the 1980's, publish the papers. We do so here as their last joint venture – or, as Tony wrote in the Preface to the Catalog, their last 'milestone on a common road'.

A few of the papers delivered at the AIA panel have subsequently been published and so have been replaced with papers of other students of Ross who were unable to be part of the original symposium. All papers, I am certain you will agree, readily fit the original charge of Image and Medium in Ancient Art and Coinage, a topic well-suited to Ross's own legacy and an appropriate expression of what we, his students, learned.

I am especially grateful to Julia Flanders for the layout of this volume, to Nancy Holloway for her close proofreading of the texts, and to my colleague and good friend, David Dapogny, for his assistance in all the illustration layouts, most especially with the complexity of mine. This volume would not have been possible without their individual efforts. And, as all the papers indicate, the students of Ross Holloway owe much to his guidance and direction as our adviser and most especially to his collegiality and good friendship since our student days.

*Susan S. Lukesh*

---

[1] Tony Hackens, Catalog of the Classical Collection: Classical Jewelry, Museum of Art, Rhode Island School of Design, 1976.

# INTRODUCTION

The papers in this volume study the subject matter and the meanings of images as well as the possible sources of some of them. Such studies, the investigation of iconography and its sister discipline iconology, have a sustained tradition in the history of art and, of course, owe much to Erwin Panofsky.[1] Stephen Bann suggests that the sustaining power of Panofsky's writing is his skill and diligence in digging out the iconographic and literary sources that unearth the meaning of a picture.[2] This talent – diligence in digging out the iconographic and literary sources – is evident in the papers presented in this volume, papers which also demonstrate how the study of images draws information and insight from a broad range of disciplines: art history and criticism, of course, as well as psychology, sociology, anthropology, and cultural theory, to name a few.

We see today, especially among the young, a shift from a text-based to a visually dependent culture, as any one in higher education would attest. Those of us in higher education find our students much more comfortable with image than the printed word; multimedia presentations of both popular and scholarly topics grow in number routinely; and visualization of information is a "hot" topic in discussions of new information delivery vehicles. Continually we must ask to what degree are images a natural form of communication, and, more importantly, do we learn to read images in the same way that we read a book? Can we say that images and text are equivalent communication systems built simply with different codes and a different grammar? Yet those of us immersed in the ancient world, a world often not far removed from pre-literate oral cultures, have long been familiar with the power of images to convey far more information than is easily expressed in words.

Leaving the ancient world, history passes into the largely illiterate middle ages when religious art spoke through images to the masses, heraldry became a language of signs, and symbols identified the shops of simple commerce. In early modern times books at first carried hand drawn ornamentation in the tradition of illuminated medieval manuscripts. But the image was not slow to assert its importance quite apart from the text. The simple woodcuts of early printed books had been replaced, by the end of the sixteenth century, by the magnificent illustrations of volumes of anatomy, geography, science (especially military technology), and Roman antiquity. Thus, today's highly visually-based learners are, in a sense, simply responding to a way of presenting information that has always been appreciated.

The use of visual tools (a.k.a. images) to impart information, in fact to truly understand data, has an interesting history described by Edward Tufte.[3] Most interesting to me are two of his examples. The first is the classic of Charles Joseph Minard, the French engineer, which shows the terrible fate of Napoleon's army in Russia ... this combination of data map and time-series, drawn in 1861, portrays the devastating losses suffered in Napoleon's Russian campaign of 1812.[4] The second example is the early use of a map to chart patterns of disease, the famous dot map of Dr. John Snow, who plotted the location of deaths from cholera in central London for September 1854.[5] Deaths were marked by dots and, in addition, the area's eleven water pumps were located by crosses. It was the presence of these water pumps, in particular the Broad Street water pump, which showed that cholera occurred almost entirely among those who lived near or drank from this pump. I cite both these examples to illustrate the power of the image over the spoken/written word. As an archaeologist I have been all too aware that the mass of seemingly trivial

---

[1] Iconography and Iconology: An Introduction to the Study of Renaissance Art in Meaning in the Visual Arts, Papers in and on Art History, 1955, Chapter 1.

[2] Meaning/Interpretation in Robert S. Nelson and Richard Schiff, eds., Critical Terms for Art History, 1996.

[3] The Visual Display of Quantitative Information, 1983; Envisioning Information, 1990; and Visual Explanations, 1997.

[4] Tufte (in note 3), 1983, p. 40.

[5] Tufte (in note 3), 1983, p. 24.

bits and pieces we excavate often, if properly arrayed, has much to say.[6]

My seeming digression into the use of visualization of data to convey information is meant to be a deliberate reminder of the information presented by the image and, hence, the power of the image, a power which the ancients knew and which we, to our peril, forget when we view ancient art. The papers in this volume speak both to the information in the image and, importantly, to the image's relationship to the medium on which it is presented, whether ancient pot, coin, sculpture, or, in one instance, the cityscape itself. Reading an image and reading a text are related activities but the understandings derived from reading an image are often far less straightforward than those derived from a printed text and certainly not as easily taught as reading text. Reading the texts describing and illuminating various images in this volume will, I believe, illustrate this point. I commend them to you.

*Susan S. Lukesh*

---

[6] Susan S. Lukesh, Expanding the Archaeologist's Toolkit: Scientific Visualization of Archaeological Data in Imaging the Past: Electronic Imaging and Computer Graphics in Museums and Archaeology, A Conference at the British Museum, London 3rd-5th November, 1994, British Museum Occasional Paper No. 114, 1996, p. 245-57.

# EARLY BRONZE AGE SICILIAN GEOMETRIC DECORATION: ITS ORIGIN AND RELATIONSHIP TO VESSEL FORM

*Susan S. Lukesh*

On the one hand, this essay owes everything to R. Ross Holloway with whom I have worked and studied for close to 35 years, specifically to his ready ability to entertain new ideas and ways of approaching the material we have excavated together. On the other hand, I am indebted to Joseph Mascheck, Professor of Fine Arts and Art History at Hofstra University, without whose advice and ideas this specific piece might not have seen the light of day.

## Introduction

The hallmark painted geometric decoration of the Early Bronze Age Sicilian Castelluccian pottery offers fertile ground for a variety of studies, and the site of La Muculufa in south central Sicily, excavated in the early 1980s, with over 100,000 sherds recovered – roughly 30% of them with painted decoration – provides an especially rich collection of material.

These fragments of pots, and the whole pots which were slowly and painstakingly put together, have furnished insights into the Castelluccian culture in south-central Sicily and the network of communities from which these and related objects were recovered. Some of the sherds from La Muculufa have formed the basis of my own attribution of a body of work to one recognizable prehistoric artist, called the Muculufa Master.[1] The study of these ceramics has also contributed to our growing understanding of socio-political organization in Early Bronze Age Sicily and the Salso River Valley and provided the potential for well-defined chronologies.

And, finally, the study of this body of material has also brought me to consideration of the origins of the Castel-

luccian motifs. Others, too, have considered possible origins of the motifs on this pottery. In particular, Sluga Messina[2] has found parallels to a number of Castelluccian motifs in the eastern Mediterranean, especially, she concludes, in the interior regions of Greece and Asia Minor, rather than in material from the coasts or outlying islands. She traces specific motifs to Iran and Asia Minor, for example the 'sun' or 'eye' and the hook/spiral (Fig. 1 & 2). Frankly, the very expanse of the area and the lack of precise chronological connections argue against drawing any significant conclusions.

Additionally, Sluga Messina has suggested that the 'Castelluccian' motifs used by modern day Algerian potters on their pots trace their history back through the millennia although the significance of the symbols has been lost. While this is possible, unless an unbroken history of use can be demonstrated, I believe that similar motifs do not necessitate a similar origin. I have argued in another forum that the common use of simple motifs around the world need not indicate a common origin.[3] And just as I would not argue that the pattern of a row of filled triangles below a horizontal band on the rim of a Pueblo pot from the 15th–16th centuries A.D. derives from those same Castelluccian motifs (on a pot of similar shape), so I am unwilling, on the basis of evidence to date, to ascribe all the

[1] Susan S. Lukesh, "The La Muculufa Master and Company: The Identification of A Workshop of Early Bronze Age Castelluccian Painters," Revue des Archeologues et Historiens d'Art de Louvain, 2, 1993, p. 9–24.

[2] G. Sluga Messina, Analisi dei motivi decorativi della ceramica da Castelluccio di Noto (Siracusa), Universita degli studi di Trieste, Facolta di Lettere e Filosofia, Istituto di Archeologia (Roma, 1983).

[3] S. S. Lukesh, Reflections on Castelluccian Material and Future Research Directions, in Brian E. McConnell, La Muculufa II Excavation and Survey 1988–1991: The Castelluccian Village and Other Areas, Archaeologia Transatlantica, XIII, 1995, p. 185–210.

correspondence noted by Sluga Messina to direct origin in the eastern Mediterranean.

The last argument of Sluga Messina's regarding the motifs of modern day Algerian potters is reminiscent of Alois Riegl's vision of an unbroken historical continuity of an underlying core of fundamental motifs and his refusal to allow the derivation of some geometric motifs from the techniques of production and the nature of materials despite the evidence of natural parallels. Riegl presented his argument in a series of lectures delivered during the winter of 1890/91 at the University of Vienna and subsequently published in 1893 in Stilfragen[4] where he argued for an historical development of ornament and against an origin which would allow the spontaneous appearance of motifs around the world. To account for such a spontaneous appearance of geometric motifs one might have to turn to a common, non-ornamental inspiration, such as textiles, basketry and wickerwork and to this Riegl was opposed.

Despite the strong case Riegl made for separating the origins of geometric design in general from weaving and basketry, there remain clear instances when specific origins can be argued, and consideration in this essay is of one instance when material and technique (here textile, basketry and wickerwork) stimulated decoration schema in another medium (Castelluccian painted pottery). These results, I argue, in the hands of at least one artist (the Muculufa Master) produced a product which far surpassed the mere reflection of the original source of inspiration and succeeded as true art. It is a consideration of this point, the possibility of just such an origin and its translation to the medium of ceramics, that is the subject of this essay.

## Semper & Riegl

Let us turn then to Alois Riegl and his book Stilfragen (published originally in 1893 and most recently in English translation in 1992 with excellent annotations by David Castriota) in which he argued against the belief that all art forms were always the direct product of materals and technique. This belief developed from the work of Gottfried Semper who, Riegl acknowledges, argued only that material and technique played a role in the genesis of art forms.

It was his followers, dubbed Semperians, who turned it into something absolute. Riegl proposed in Stilfragen to "address the most fundamental and harmful of misconceptions and preconceptions that hinder research"[5] and suggested that he would "demonstrate that not only is there no cogent reason for assuming a priori that the oldest geometric decorations were executed in any particular technique, least of all weaving [in which term Riegl included basketry], but that the earliest, genuinely historical monuments we possess in fact contradict this assumption."[6] This attempt to eliminate "the one principle that has ruled the entire field of art theory for the past quarter century: the absolute equation of textile patterns with the surface decoration or ornament"[7] in some ways succeeded far too well, inhibiting attempts to search in specific instances for such an equation. Riegl states in the introduction to his book that he wishes "to reduce the importance of textile decoration to the level it deserves."[8]

Ultimately, of course, Riegl was arguing for the case of progressive development of ornamental patterns, according to principles of historical methodology and in such a fashion as to reflect relationships and interactions among historical communities. He mentions the "haste of scholars to assure us that they would never be so foolish and naive as to believe, for example, that one culture could have ever copied a 'simple' meander band from another [and their] repeated apologies whenever they do venture to assert even a loose connection between, shall we say, the sylized two-dimensional vegetal motifs current in two geographic areas."[9] He suggests that the "materialist interpretation of the origin of arts is nothing other than Darwinism imposed upon an intellectual discipline."[10] Semperian thinking, he argues, has led to insistence

- that the few basic motifs of the Geometric style occur in the same manner among practically all prehistoric and contemporary primitive cultures in Europe and Asia, in Africa as well as in America and Polynesia and

---

[4] A. Riegl, Problems of Style Foundations for History of Ornament, translated by Evelyn Kain, Annotations and Introduction by David Castriota, Preface by Henry Zerner, 1992.

[5] Ibidem, p. 5.

[6] Ibidem, p. 5.

[7] Ibidem, p. 5.

[8] Ibidem, p. 6.

[9] Ibidem, p. 3.

[10] Ibidem, p. 4.

- that therefore the Geometric style originated spontaneously throughout the entire world and
- that its origins must be a common source in all cultures – hence textiles which people share in common.

Although, in fact, Riegl (and Semper) believed that technique and material played a formative role at a more advanced stage but not at the very inception of artistic activity, Riegl's eloquent argument in this volume has led to an insistence, in some areas, that motifs never originated independently and spontaneously but always derived from other areas. Here specifically I reference the Sicilian Bronze Age, the study of whose decoration patterns has led some to conclude that some complex patterns *must* have been influenced by similar ones discovered among their neighbors in the eastern Mediterranean, implicitly supporting the belief that nothing originated in Sicily – it was all derived from their neighbors to the East.

The strength of Riegl's argument against techno-materialist origins for geometric patterns led to the denial, in some circles, of techno-materialist origins for any instances of geometric patterning. One of Riegl's aims in his volume was to disprove the techno-materialist origin of geometric decoration in general; my purpose here is not to prove Riegl wrong but simply to consider a possible direct association between textile, basketry, and wickerwork and Sicilian Early Bronze Age Castelluccian ceramic decoration. This painted decoration remains, I believe, as a reminder of the origin of the motifs (much as Petrie found vestigial handles in painted wavy lines on an albeit strategic part of a pot). I argue further that the subsequent development of these decoration patterns in the work of the Castelluccian painter, the Muculufa Master, far surpassed the limitations of influence from textile and basketry production and became art. This final point is one which might have allowed Riegl to accept a technical-materialist origin of some geometric decoration as it demonstrates convincingly the artist's ability to break the bounds of craft production and create something attaining to fine art.

## Castelluccian motifs and techno-materialist sources

Flinders Petrie, whose presentation of the vestigial handles I just mentioned, was a contemporary of Riegl. Riegl was born in 1858 and died in 1905; Petrie, born five years earlier in 1853, outlasted him by far, living until 1942. As the Edwards Professor of Egyptology at University College, London, Petrie delivered a course of lectures on Egyptian Decorative Art which were published in 1895.[11] This professorship was created and Petrie appointed after Amelia Edwards' death in April 1892, and so Petrie must have delivered these lectures within the next couple of years, just a few years after Riegl delivered his lectures in Vienna. In Petrie's lectures, he proposed to limit his "view to the historical development of the various motifs or elements of decoration."[12] Although Petrie made no attempt to propose a history of ornament or even Egyptian ornament, he subscribed to a view with which Riegl would have agreed: "It is very difficult or almost impossible to point out decoration which is proved to have originated independently, and not to have been copied from the Egyptian stock."[13] In support of his argument against continual re-invention of motifs, he writes "The very fact that the locality and date of an object of unknown origin can be so closely predicted by its style and feeling in design, is the best proof how continuous is the history and evolution of ornament, and how little new invention has to do with it."[14] Nonetheless, he indicated his belief that, "the influence of the modes of work in weaving and basket-work have had much to do with the uniformity of patterns in different countries."[15]

This small volume of charming lectures was reissued in 1972 and provides an interesting counterpoint to Riegl, interesting especially since both men discuss the work of the American W. G. Goodyear who, in his book The Grammar of the Lotus,[16] was the "first to argue that all antique vegetal ornament, and a good deal more, was a continuation of ancient Egyptian lotus ornament."[17] Apparently Riegl and Petrie were unaware of each other's work at this time.

---

[11] W.M.F. Petrie, Egyptian Decorative Art: A Course of Lectures Delivered at the Royal Institution, 1895.

[12] Ibidem, p. 2.

[13] Ibidem, p. 5.

[14] Ibidem, p. 8–9.

[15] Ibidem, p. 5–6.

[16] W.G. Goodyear, The Grammar of the Lotus. A New History of Classical Ornament as a Development of Sun Worship, 1891.

[17] Riegl, cit. in note 5, p. 7.

As we move into considering the reflections of weaving, plaiting and basketry as well as other natural forms in Castelluccian painted decoration, it is useful to consider briefly the specific parallels offered by Petrie.

Petrie addressed the sources of decoration (geometrical, natural, structural and symbolic) and in his consideration of structural decoration he points out how the pots drying in the sun before firing in Egyptian pottery yards of his day are held together by rough palm fiber cord. Out of the accidental marking on the clay from the cord, he suggests, came a pattern he terms the twist or guilloche (Fig. 3), which he derived from the rope pattern rather than a "chain of coils or wave patterns." Ever the archaeologist, he develops from the evidence of screens behind the figures of owners of early tombs the idea that some patterns were made "by binding the fibers into bundles, and so making a kind of open work, which may well have led to the pattern of connected rhomb (Fig. 4)."[18] Certainly we see such patterns on Castelluccian pots. In the first instance cited, Petrie has translated a marking made by production techniques to a later pattern; in the second he found the inspiration for a pattern in basketry or wickerwork. The checker patterns of geometric design, ubiquitous to Castelluccian pots, derive, according to Petrie, unmistakably from plaiting and weaving, a source of inspiration I am convinced served the Castelluccian potters as well.

Feathers and the variety of their forms, Petrie argued, are "one source of simple pattern that has been little noticed."[19] He offers a number of examples of feathers, three of which find immediate reflection in Castelluccian pottery (Fig. 5 corresponds to Fig. 6 and 7; Fig. 8 and 10 correspond to Fig. 9 and 11, respectively). He traces a history of decorative feather motifs on Egyptian material from the obvious to examples where the pattern was corrupted and the origin as featherwork probably lost.

Finally, I mention Petrie's derivation of rhombic-form frets from basketwork, as seen in the screen behind a figure at Giza (Fig. 12), and his attribution of the development of frets to the translation of spirals to textiles (and basketwork). The source of the spiral has been attributed, Petrie related, to the development of the lotus pattern although, he added, it is known in every variety of treatment without any trace of connection to the lotus.[20] Certainly it is seen on Castelluccian pottery (Fig. 13 and 14). Petrie, in his discourse on the spiral, offers a small vignette which tells much about his approach to interpretation of symbolic meanings:

> It has been said to represent the wanderings of the soul; why, or how, is not specified; nor why some souls should wander in circular spirals, others in oval spirals, some in spirals with ends, others in spirals that are endless. And what a soul was supposed to do when on the track of a triple diverging spiral, how could it go two ways at once, or which line it was to take – all these difficulties suggest that the theorist's soul was on a remarkable spiral.[21]

But we need not rely on Petrie's work to find possible sources in weaving, plaiting and basketry for many Castelluccian motifs (nor, in fact, on Castelluccian pots to demonstrate other such borrowings). Recourse to current texts on weaving, plaiting and basketry gives us any manner of parallels. I illustrate a few here.

Wickerwork as illustrated in The Complete Book of Baskets and Basketry[22] shows us a simple wavy line pattern (Fig. 15) which is echoed on many Castelluccian pots (Fig. 16). From baskets again we see patterns formed when bases are created (Fig. 17 and 18); these are echoed repeatedly in the painted patterns on the inside of pedestalled bowls (Fig. 19) as on the bottom of pots (Fig. 20). Plaiting as opposed to coiled, rush or twined baskets offers some very expressive examples, one in progress (Fig. 21) and one complete (Fig. 22). Petrie's own plates of decorative patterns of the ancient world[23] gives direct parallels (Fig. 23 and 24). And basketry knots (Fig. 25) are also reflected in ancient patterns as Fig. 26 shows.

An example of twill patterning (Fig. 27)[24] can be placed beside a fragment from La Muculufa (Fig. 28) which seems a direct reflection of the pattern.

---

[18] Petrie, cit. in note 12, 94.

[19] Ibidem, p. 50.

[20] Ibidem, p. 17.

[21] Ibidem.

[22] D. Wright, The Complete Book of Baskets and Basketry, 1983 edition published by David & Charles Inc., North Pomfret, Vermont.

[23] W.M.F. Petrie, Decorative Patterns of the Ancient World, re-edition 1995.

[24] S. Glashausser and C. Westfall, Plaiting Step-by-Step, 1976.

And when we turn to band weaving[25] we can see how the small looms used for weaving long strips would generate patterns readily paralleled in the painted patterns of Castelluccian pottery. This illustration of eight different band patterns (Fig. 29) finds easy reflection on Castelluccian pots. The pattern third from the left finds direct comparison with the motif on the neck band on a fragmentary cup (Fig. 30). The sixth pattern from the left is a ubiquitous Castelluccian neck pattern as well as for 'supports' of the bowl on many cups; see, for example, Fig. 31 and 32.

And finally the pattern of hatched diamonds in a row (Fig. 33) produced on a compact inkle loom is found throughout Castelluccian painted decoration (Fig. 34 and 35).

Other than the example of the fiber cord on drying pots, Petrie offers no way in which or reason for the sources he cited to be translated to geometric motifs in other media. I have presented specific illustrations not because I believe that those who decorated Castelluccian pots were bereft of imagination and required inspiration from another medium but because I believe that the decorative motifs from weaving and wickerwork were intimately tied to the pots. In the first instance, ceramic vessels performed a similar function to baskets – carrier of foodstuffs. In the second instance, I suggest that woven or wickerwork bands surrounded the necks and supported the bodies of Sicilian Early Bronze Age pots at one point in their history and so the decoration patterns and schema became associated with these pots, long after the original association may have been lost.

## The Muculufa Master

But if we can be convinced that one source of inspiration for Castelluccian painted decoration is the materials and techniques of weaving and wickerwork, I also suggest that in the same Castelluccian painted pottery we see instances when the use of these motifs has far surpassed the original inspiration and produced painted pots approaching art.

Just as Riegl doubted "that weaving or textile art provided the immediate source for the Dipylon Style, since its decorative vocabulary can be traced back consistently in Greek vase painting to products of the tenth or eleventh centuries B.C.",[26] so I would argue that the work of the Muculufa Master was not directly inspired by weaving or wickerwork.

The pot illustrated here is the name vase of the Muculufa Master (Fig. 36). My identification of this painter followed the detailed examination of a number of reconstructed pots from La Muculufa and fragmentary vessels and sherds from other sites, Xiboli, Monte San Giuliano, and Casalicchio-Agnone. It was based on three critical points: design composition (structure), selection and interpretation of particular motifs (form), and execution of particular motifs (technique). The material reviewed permitted, for the first time, the identification of distinct hands among painters of Castelluccian pottery. Beginning with the name vase of the Muculufa Master, I identified fragmentary examples of pots which reflect the same selection of motifs, the same overall comprehension of balance in the design composition, suggesting a common set of structural rules, and even the same technique or execution of motifs. Fig. 37, a fragment of a smaller pot, illustrates, I believe, the hand of the Master on another pot – even in this small piece there is a sense of a very balanced composition and an equal if not greater sureness of hand. Figure 38 illustrates a fragment of an amphora whose motif selection and design composition strongly argue for the same workshop if not the same artisan as our Master. In addition, a group of fragmentary cups (Fig. 39 and 40), while not currently used to identify distinct hands, reinforces the close relationship among painters of pots found at La Muculufa, Casalicchio-Agnone, Xiboli, Monte San Giuliano, Canticaglione, and Canicatti, all sites in or close to the Salso River valley. Finally, Fig. 41 illustrates a partially reconstructed amphora whose composition is well laid out with alternating metopes of multiple angular lines and vertically positioned angular lines adorned with spirals rather than 'berries'. This second motif has three lines in the central panel or metope and only two on the left and right versions. As on the name vase, the handle area on the neck is solid black. The neck and body are delimited by a set of three unadorned zigzag lines; the body is filled with the same multiple line pattern used in the neck metopes; and the handle area on the body carries the hatched band seen on many vases, including the name vase.

[25] H. and S. Tacker, Band Weaving, The Techniques, Looms, and Uses for Woven Bands, 1974.

[26] Riegl, cit. in note 5, annotation I, p. 309.

The execution of the motifs, however, is less fine and the selection and organization of motifs less complex than on the name vase. In fact, the size of the metopes on the neck, which are filled with the same pattern on the lower body, changes the impression of the vessel to one primarily decorated with one motif, occasionally relieved by sets of zigzag lines; this is quite different from the design structure on the name vase. While this amphora was not executed by the Muculufa Painter, it is likely that it was created with the knowledge of the name vase tradition and the manufacturer's 'shop'; that is, the painter was familiar with the set of structural rules governing the design composition of the pots discussed above, as well as the individual selection of motifs. This amphora was executed much more quickly and much less expertly.

## Conclusion

We have come a long way from pots whose decoration, I suggest, imitated or reflected basket precursors or ceramic precursors with basketry or woven supports. I have attempted to demonstrate how the techno-materialist sources for the antecedents of the Muculufa Master and Company have been translated in the hands of some talented artisans and developed well beyond their origins. And developed, in fact, into a class of painted pottery that takes its place beside some of the best of the Minoan, Mycenaean and Greek Geometric painted pottery.

The tradition of Early Bronze Age Sicilian painted pottery with the recognition of a master craftsman and his workshop enlightens us in terms of socio-political organization but also demonstrates the development of art in an early not yet well-known period. This tradition, I suggest to you, deserves a proud place in Bronze Age Mediterranean studies.

**Fig. 1.** Castelluccian sherd, La Muculufa.

**Fig. 2.** Castelluccian sherd, La Muculufa.

**Fig. 3.** Guilloche, after Petrie, Egyptian Decoration, Fig. 170.

**Fig. 4.** Connected rhombs, after Petrie, Egyptian Decoration, Fig. 172.

**Fig. 5.** Feather pattern from XIth dynasty coffin, after Petrie, Egyptian Decoration, Fig. 91.

**Fig. 6.** Castelluccian cup, La Muculufa.

**Fig. 7.** Castelluccian cup, La Muculufa.

**Fig. 8.** Feather pattern from XIth dynasty coffin, after Petrie, Egyptian Decoration, Fig. 92.

**Fig. 9.** Castelluccian sherd, La Muculufa.

**Fig. 10.** Feather pattern from XIth dynasty coffin, after Petrie, Egyptian Decoration, Fig. 94.

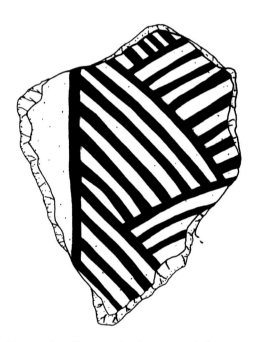

**Fig. 11.** Castelluccian sherd, La Muculufa.

**Fig. 12.** Fret of rhombic form, Vth dynasty, after Petrie, Egyptian Decoration, Fig. 60.

**Fig. 13.** Castelluccian sherd, La Muculufa.

**Fig. 14.** Castelluccian sherd, La Muculufa.

Fig. 15. Melanu baskets from Sarawak, Wright, color plate 2.

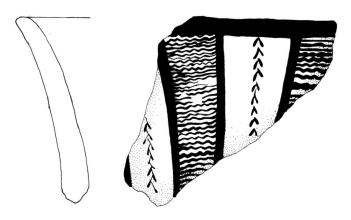

Fig. 16. Castelluccian sherd from foot of pedestalled pot, La Muculufa.

Fig. 17. Beginning weaving of basketry base, Wright, illus. 97.

Fig. 18. Beginning weaving of basketry base, Wright, illus. 103.

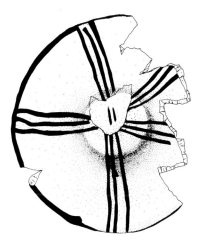

Fig. 19. Castelluccian sherd, inside bowl of pedestalled pot, La Muculufa.

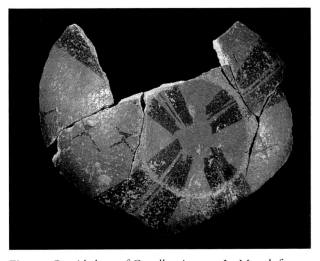

Fig. 20. Outside base of Castelluccian pot, La Muculufa.

**Fig. 22.** Plaited basket, Wright, illus. 228.

**Fig. 21.** Plaiting in progress, Wright, illus. 135.

**Fig. 23.** Six twist from Kincizha, Dalmatia ca. 300 A.D., after Petrie, Decorative Patterns, XLIV H65.

**Fig. 24.** Quadruple twist, Syro-Hittite cylinder, Petrie, Decorative Patterns, XLIV MH1.

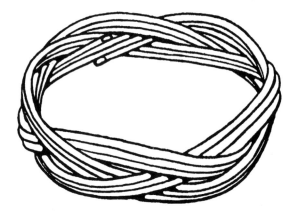

**Fig. 25.** Knot from sailor's or scout's lanyard, Wright, illus. 155.

**Fig. 26.** Double twist, Canterbury, ca. 650 A.D. after Petrie, Decorative Patterns, XLII F10.

**Fig. 27.** Antique domed basket with twill patterning, India, Glashausser and Westfall, p. 25.

**Fig. 28.** Castelluccian cup, La Muculufa.

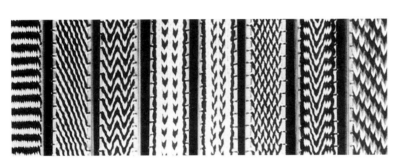

**Fig. 29.** Basic twining-loom band patterns, Tacker and Tacker, ill. 6–17.

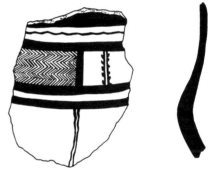

**Fig. 30.** Castelluccian cup, La Muculufa.

**Fig. 31.** Castelluccian cup, La Muculufa.

**Fig. 32.** Castelluccian cup, La Muculufa.

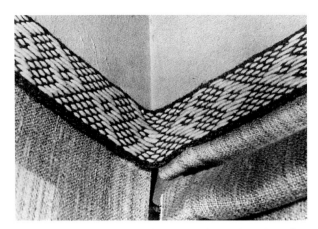

**Fig. 33.** Inkle band with pick-up design, Tacker and Tacker, ill. 8–17.

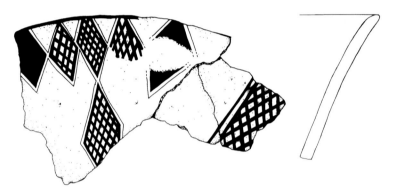

**Fig. 34.** Castelluccian sherd, inside bowl of pedestalled pot, La Muculufa.

**Fig. 35.** Castelluccian sherd, inside bowl of ped-estalled pot, La Muculufa.

**Fig. 36.** La Muculufa Master name vase.

**Fig. 37.** Castelluccian sherd, La Muculufa.

**Fig. 38.** Castelluccian sherd, La Muculufa.

**Fig. 39.** Castelluccian cup, La Muculufa.

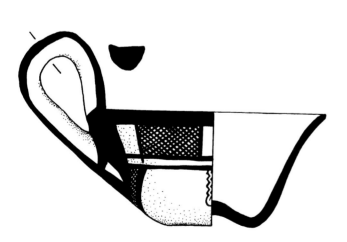

**Fig. 40.** Castelluccian cup, La Muculufa.

**Fig. 41.** Reconstructed Castelluccian pot, La Muculufa.

# EXEKIAS' "SUICIDE OF AJAX" AND THE PROBLEM OF SOCIO-POLITICAL SYMBOLISM IN GREEK VASE-PAINTING

*Joseph J. Basile*

This article is dedicated to the memory of Prof. Tony Hackens, and to his friend and colleague Prof. R. Ross Holloway. It is based, in part, on a paper read at the 98th Annual Meeting of the Archaeological Institute of America in New York City in December of 1996 (at the Gold Medal Colloquium honoring Professor Holloway entitled "Image and Medium in Ancient Art and Coinage"), and on the article "Exekias, Ajax, and the Classical Tradition," published in Forays (the faculty journal of the Maryland Institute, College of Art), Spring 1996, p. 7 ff.

Exekias was one of several ancient Greek artists who must be numbered among the great geniuses of the Western tradition. Some art historians have considered him to be one of the few artists from any period who so excelled in his particular medium that he may have played a role in its obsolescence (for his skill could not be exceeded); recently it has been suggested by others that he also excelled in the creation of art that had complex political and social content. In many ways, Exekias resembles the great pioneers of modern art, not only challenging the artistic climate of his day but also, perhaps, conventional political views. This paper will examine the supposed political nature of some of Exekias' work, and relate these "theories of meaning" to one of his most famous vases: the Boulogne amphora depicting the suicide of Telamonian Ajax.

The first aspect of Exekias' talent – that he was one of the greatest artists in his medium, the black figure style of Archaic Attic vase painting – is an opinion that has long been held by certain art historians. In the black figure style, limited as it was by the necessity of depicting form and ornament essentially as two-dimensional silhouette, Exekias achieved nearly all there was to achieve. By the end of his relatively short career Athenian artists had for the most part abandoned the black figure style in favor of red figure, a technique which allowed greater detail of depiction. Some believe that the talent exhibited by Exekias had in many ways rendered the black figure style obsolete,

and hastened the advent of red figure – indeed, many scholars suspect the innovator of the red figure technique to be the Andokides Painter, a student of Exekias who learned his lessons all too well.[1] None could hope to surpass Exekias' accomplishments in the old style, so artists like the Andokides Painter left it in favor of the new.

Details of Exekias' career can be found in a number of sources[2] – we will only summarize the key points here. His oeuvre includes some 12 vases which he signed as painter, and a dozen other fragments attributed to his hand on a stylistic basis, though he also painted plaques and was a talented potter, signing six vases in this capacity.[3] Indeed, although Exekias' "monumental" figures, attention to detail, and concern with potential (as opposed

---

[1] J. Boardman, Athenian Black Figure Vases, 1974, p. 103–105 (hereafter ABFV); J. Hurwit, The Art and Culture of Early Greece, 700–480 BC, 1985, (hereafter Hurwit 1985) p. 282.

[2] See J.D. Beazley, Attic Black Figure: A Sketch, Proceedings of the British Academy 14, 1928, p. 17–21 and 29–31 (hereafter referred to as ABFS); W. Technau, Exekias, Bilder Griechischer Vasen, Heft 9, 1936, p. 7 ff.; J.D. Beazley, The Development of Attic Black Figure, 1951, p. 63–72, 112–113, and 119 (hereafter referred to as Development); J. Boardman, Painted Funerary Plaques and Some Remarks on Prothesis, BSA 50, 1955, p. 63–65; P. Clement, Geryon and Others in Los Angeles, Hesperia 24, 1955, p. 8 ff; J.D. Beazley, Attic Black-Figure Vase-Painters, 1956, p. 133, 143–147, 686–687, and 714 (hereafter referred to as ABV); P. Arias, A History of Greek Vase Painting, translated and revised by B. Shefton, 1962, p. 300 ff, pls. 16–18, and figs. 59–65; H. Cahn, Exekiasfragmente, AntK 5, 1962, p. 77 ff; M. Moore, Horses by Exekias, AJA 72, 1968, p. 357 ff.; J. Beazley, Paralipomena, 1971, p. 61 (hereafter referred to as Paralipomena); ABFV, p. 56–58, ill. 96–106 and frontispiece; J. Boardman, Exekias, AJA 82, 1978, p. 11 ff.; M. Moore, Exekias and Telamonian Ajax, AJA 84, 1980, p. 417 ff.; etc.

[3] Development, p. 70–71; ABV, 143–147; Paralipomena, p. 61.

15

to overt) action must place him among the greatest of the black figure painters,[4] it has been argued that he was equally important as a potter, responsible perhaps for the early development of the Type A cup, the Type A belly amphora, and the Type B amphora, as well as the invention of the calyx crater.[5] Exekias achieved all of this despite a relatively short career in the Athenian potter's quarter – his painted vases are typically dated between 545 and 530 BC[6] – and was probably the most influential of all the Archaic Attic black figure vase painters.

That Exekias' art contained subtle political and social statements, of sophistication and complexity not often seen in ancient art, is however an idea that has only recently been explored. The British classicist and art historian Sir John Boardman was among the first to begin analyzing Archaic Greek art, especially Athenian art and the painted vases of Exekias, for political content. In the 1960s, Boardman and other scholars, such as Martin Robertson, began to express concern for the field of vase painter studies, in the generation after Beazley.[7] Could the discipline maintain its vitality with its focus still mainly on attribution? The response was an attempt to define "…painters as artists in the fuller sense of the word…" by seeking to arrive at the meaning of their art.[8] In his 1978 article "Exekias" for the American Journal of Archaeology, Boardman examined the subject matter of Exekias' painted scenes, suggesting that the statistical regularity with which certain ones appeared – like those dealing with Herakles, the Di-

oskouroi, Theseus and his sons, and the Trojan War scenes of Achilles and Ajax – represented allusions to contemporary events.[9] In Exekias' time, the tyrant Peisistratos was twice returned to power in Athens by means of stratagem. This meant the supplanting of the traditional power elite (the aristocratic faction) and the establishment of a new and untested order; in the language of Aristotle, this new order was an extra-constitutional tyranny, whose constituency was essentially the hoplites and lower classes, continuing the inexorable march of the Athenians towards class egalitarianism and democracy.[10] Herodotus, who was closer to the event chronologically, depicts the struggle rather as a regional/factional one between the "plains" party of Lycurgos, the "shore" party of Megakles the Alkmaeonid, and Peisistratos' own people from "beyond the hills."[11] Wherever the truth may lie, many of Athens' aristocratic families found themselves deprived of traditional rights and prerogatives, and people of all classes soon came to live in a polis with a developing bureaucracy and new governmental structures which demanded more of its citizens. This then is the critical historical context surrounding the artistic career of Exekias, and Sir John Boardman suggests that at least some of his painted vases reflect these turbulent times.

Exekias' own political leanings – if he had any – are not at first clear in Boardman's interpretation. Originally, Exekias may have been a supporter of the Peisistratid faction; Boardman sees Exekias' scenes of Herakles as a positive allusion to the tyranny of Peisistratos, who becomes a kind of "new Herakles" in the art of Athens.[12] This era was a "golden age" of culture in Archaic Attica, and painters like Exekias prospered under the restored regime.[13]

---

[4] ABFV, p. 56–58; B.H. Fowler, The Centaur's Smile: Pindar and the Archaic Aesthetic, Ancient Greek Art and Iconography, ed. W. Moon, 1983, p. 163; Hurwit 1985, p. 259–261 and 271–272.

[5] O. Broneer, A Calyx-krater by Exekias, Hesperia 6, 1937, p. 469 ff.; Development, 70–71; ABV, 143–147; Paralipomena, p. 61; ABFV, p. 56–58 and fig. 103; E.E. Bell, An Exekian Puzzle in Portland: Further Light In the Relationship between Exekias and Group E, Ancient Greek Art and Iconography, ed. W.G. Moon, 1983, p. 75 and 84; W.G. Moon, The Priam Painter: Some Iconographic and Stylistic Considerations, Ancient Greek Art and Iconography, ed. W.G. Moon, 1983, p. 98.

[6] Technau, cit. in note 2, p. 7; ABFS, p. 6; ABFV, p. 57. For an attempt to establish a relative chronology for the major vases and fragments attributed to Exekias, see Moore 1968, p. 357–368 (especially p. 367).

[7] J. Boardman, Exekias, AJA, 1978, p. 11–25

[8] Ibidem.

[9] p. 11–25.

[10] Athenaion Politeia, 13.4–15.3; see also R. Sealey, A History of the Greek City States 700–338 BC, 1976, p. 126–127 and 134–142.

[11] 1.59–1.64; see also Sealey p. 123–128.

[12] Boardman, cit in note 8, p. 13–16. Earlier, Boardman had argued that scenes of Athena introducing Herakles to Olympos on her chariot referred to the ruse Peisistratos employed to have himself returned to power after the collapse of the first tyranny; see Herakles, Peisistratos, and Sons, RA 1972, p. 57–72; Hurwit 1985 p. 247, n. 46. Contra see D. Williams, Ajax, Odysseus, and the Arms of Achilles, AntK 23, 1980, p. 144, n. 55; Moon, cit. in note 5 p. 97–118.

[13] Hurwit 1985, p. 246–247 and 249–250.

On the painted vases of Exekias, scenes of Herakles, Theseus and his sons, and even the Dioskouroi reflect Athens' new prosperity, increased feelings of patriotism and unity in Attica, and important Peisistratid reforms like those of the Eleusinian mysteries (into which Herakles and the Dioskouroi were incorporated as "coopted" Athenian heroes).[14] Trojan War heroes may refer to Athens' new connections to the performance of the Homeric epics in Athenian festivals, and Ajax may symbolize territorial assertions regarding the island of Salamis, that hero's home (as does, perhaps, the scene of Herakles battling Triton, which becomes popular in Athenian vase painting and sculpture at this time).[15] He may have had a change of heart, however, with the third Peisistratid tyranny, born as it was with the violence at Pallene, and resulting as it did in the increased role of the less-than-popular sons of Peisistratos, Hippias and Hipparchos. Seemingly, Exekias was unsure of this new order, as were many other Athenians, and, according to Boardman's now-classic argument, chided the defenders of Athens by means of his painted images – specifically, the Vatican Amphora showing Achilles and Ajax playing a board game (Fig. 1)[16] – for allowing the final plot to restore Peisistratos to unfold under their noses.[17] The full meaning of the scene on the Vatican Amphora is unclear, and it is widely agreed that the theme of Achilles and Ajax at play may very well be one that Exekias invented out of whole cloth.[18] It is also usually assumed, however, that the moment depicted here is one of non-vigilance – the non-vigilance that resulted in the successful raid of the Trojans on the Achaean camp and the burning of their ships. Thus, Boardman suggests that Exekias is making an allusion – one which would have been abundantly clear to his contemporary audience – and his Vatican Amphora scene refers in fact to the non-

chalance of the aristocratic faction at Pallene (and its concomitant violence).[19] If this theory is in fact correct, then Exekias is a remarkable artist indeed – one innovating at both the technical and the iconographic/symbolic level.

Boardman's attempts to recover symbolic meaning in Archaic art were based in earlier work, and were not confined to the painted vases of Exekias.[20] Indeed, an important early focus was on the monumental architectural and sculptural programs of Peisistratos and the symbolic value of the Peisistratid building program on the Athenian Acropolis.[21] His arguments regarding painted scenes on vases – especially ones depicting Herakles and scenes of the Trojan War – have become the most well-known, however, and have engendered a number of studies by other scholars which also attempt to discern political content in the art of the Peisistratid era. For instance, a study of the opus of the Priam Painter has been attempted, as has an examination of the evolution of scenes depicting Nereus and Triton, using the framework suggested by Boardman.[22] Similar approaches have been taken with the sculptural decoration of the Siphnian Treasury,[23] and possible allusions to the ancestors of the Peisistratid line in painted vases and other sources.[24] These attempts have been received by scholars with varying degrees of acceptance.

The limitations of Boardman's approach – which must contain speculative elements as it attempts to reconstruct an ancient "mindset" – have prompted some to be critical of his studies and those of his followers; this is reasonable and only to be expected. While some detractors have questioned the whole enterprise as being too reliant on interpretation, others have concentrated on specific details, arguing for instance that Boardman does not make it

---

[14] J. Boardman, Herakles, Peisistratos, and Eleusis, JHS 95, 1975, p. 1 ff.; Hurwit 1985, p. 247, n. 46.

[15] R. Glynn, Herakles, Nereus, and Triton: A Study of Iconography in Sixth Century Athens, AJA 85, 1981, p. 121 ff.; Hurwit 1985 p. 247, n. 46. Contra see Moore, Exekias, cit. in note 2, p. 417 ff.; Williams, cit. in note 12 p. 143–144.

[16] Vatican 344; see ABV p. 145, no. 13.

[17] Boardman, cit. in note 7, p. 18–24; Hurwit 1985 p. 259–260 and n. 61.

[18] It has been suggested, however, that such an episode may have been part of the so-called "cyclic" poems; see Williams, p. 144, n. 55.

[19] Boardman, cit. in note 7, p. 21–24; Hurwit 1985, p. 260 and n. 61. Contra see Williams, cit. in note 12, p. 144, n. 55.

[20] For instance, "Herakles, Delphi, and Kleisthenes of Sikyon," RA 1978, p. 227 ff.

[21] Boardman, cit. in note 12, p. 57 ff.; Boardman, cit. in note 14, p. 1 ff.; Hurwit 1985, p. 246–247 and n. 46.

[22] Glynn, cit. in note 15, p. 121–132.

[23] L.V. Watrous, The Sculptural Program of the Siphnian Treasury, AJA 86, 1982, p. 159–172.

[24] H.A. Shapiro, Painting, Politics, and Genealogy: Peisistratos and the Neleids, Ancient Greek Art and Iconography, ed. W.G. Moon, 1983, p. 87–96.

clear how and why certain scenes are meant to be read as in favor of or against the Peisistratid regime.[25] Still others have argued that vase painters could not have had such lofty concerns as political commentary (or even an awareness as to which scenes would make vases desirable in certain markets, like Etruria), that they never had significant control over the production of their painted scenes, or that the myths of the Greeks were too "tragic" to be so manipulated.[26] All this having been said, the value of Boardman's approach is just that: it is a creative, innovative approach – just one of many – that makes an attempt to arrive at symbolic meaning in Archaic Greek art based on an interpretation of visual evidence in relation to the historical and political context. It needn't provide us with correct answers, only with possible answers. In this respect, the most reasonable reaction to Boardman's ideas has probably been that of H.A. Shapiro, who has suggested that we can apply such theoretical frameworks if we are careful and critical – we mustn't envision a cadre of vase painters in the employ of the Athenian tyrants, churning out their propaganda messages, but rather a select number of thoughtful artists (principal of whom may have been Exekias) who were aware of the political and religious climate around them and reflected that climate in their art.[27] Taken in this light, an attempt to arrive at a "myth-symbolism" in certain painted scenes seems neither radical nor misguided; instead, it constitutes just one way to look at the works of a significant artist like Exekias.

Within the context of Boardman's approach, then, this paper will argue that another illustration of the "double" nature of Exekias' artistic genius is his amphora depicting, on one side, the death of the hero Ajax by suicide. It is currently at the Musée des Beaux-Arts et d'Archéologie, Boulogne-sur-Mer (Boulogne 558), (Fig. 2)[28] and dates perhaps from the beginning of his career.[29] Along with his scenes of Dionysos and the Pirates (the Munich Kylix),[30] Achilles slaying the Amazon queen Penthesilea (the London Amphora),[31] and Ajax and Achilles on the amphora in the Vatican, the Boulogne vase must be numbered among the great masterpieces of world art.

The suicide of Ajax was a mythological episode familiar to all Greeks. The mighty Ajax, son of Telamon and king of Salamis, was a Greek warrior in the expedition against Troy. In battle, he was second only to Achilles himself, but he was also simple, stubborn, and proud. Upon the death of Achilles, Ajax (who had recovered the body of his friend only after fierce fighting) desired his comrade's fantastic armor – crafted as it was by the god Hephaistos – as a spoil of war. However, clever Odysseus (with the help of his patroness, Athena) beguiled the Greeks, and the armor was awarded to the wily king of Ithaca. Ajax, his pride injured, resorted to the only course left to the shamed warrior-noble: he committed suicide, by jumping on his own sword. While Ajax appears in Archaic art before Exekias,[32] he was treated in a special way in the art of this painter, and appears in contexts in which he had never appeared before. This fact is an important one to recognize before embarking upon any study of the images of Ajax on Exekias' vases.

Exekias' artistic genius is fully realized in the Boulogne vase. The piece is a type B amphora decorated with a group of youths in a chariot on side B. On side A we see

---

[25] Williams, cit. in note 12, p. 144 and n. 55; Hurwit 1985, p. 260 and n. 61.

[26] Williams, cit. in note 12, p. 144, Moon, cit. in note 5, p. 97.

[27] Cit. in note 24, p. 95.

[28] E. Pottier, Album archéologique des musées de province, 1890–1891, pl. 16, 3; G. Perrot and Ch. Chipiez, Histoire de l'art dans l'antiquité, 1911–1914, vol. 10, p. 199; E. Pfuhl, Malerei und Zeichnung der Griechen, 1923, fig. 234; ABS, pl. 7; Technau, cit. in note 2, pl. 24; E. Buschor, Griechische Vasen, 1940, p. 119; Beazley Development, pl. 32, 1; ABV, p. 145, no. 18; Paralipomena, p. 60; F. Brommer, Vasenlisten zur griechischen Heldensage, 3., erweiterte Auflage, 1973, p. 380, n. A1 (hereafter referred to as Vasenlisten); ABFV, fig. 101.

[29] Dated by vase shape, type of ornament (opposed lotuses and palmettes, linked in a chain), and perhaps the horses (on side B) to just after 440, at the beginning of Exekias' career when certain aspects of his style were closer to the so-called "Group E" painters. See Moore, Horses cit. in note 2, p. 357–358, 360, and 367; Bell, cit. in note 5, p. 75.

[30] Munich 2044 (J. 339); see ABV, p. 146, no. 21.

[31] London B 210; see ABV, p. 144, no. 7.

[32] For instance on bronze shield-bands (E. Kunze, Archaische Schildbänder, Deutsches archäologisches Institut, Olympische Forschungen 2, 1950, p. 154–156), the famous Foce de Sele metopes (P. Zancani Montuoro, Heraion alla foce de Sele I, Altre metope del Primo Thesauros, Atti e memorie della Società Magna Grecia, n.s. 5, 1964, p. 73–76), Corinthian Orientalizing pottery (J.E. Henle, Greek Myths: A Vase Painter's Notebook, 1973, p. 144), and various black and red figure vases (Vasenlisten, p. 380–381).

the famed scene of Ajax's suicide from the lost epic the Aithiopis – not the gory moment of his death but as he prepares for death, steadying his sword, hilt buried in the ground.[33] His javelins, helmet, and shield are laid out before him; behind, a palm tree – symbolic of the exotic setting of western Asia – seems to weep.[34] Unbelievably, Exekias was able to display, in a relatively small pictorial field, expression and emotion in the severely limited idiom of the Black Figure style: Ajax is pensive, saddened, angered; but resolved.[35] He knows what he must do, what honor demands. No phony sentiment or bloodied corpse here – Exekias' style is one of subtlety and power at the same time.

As argued above, it has usually been the Vatican Amphora, which shows Ajax and Achilles engaged in a board game, that is cited as the "typical" example of political consciousness in Exekias' painted vases. Boardman saw this scene as a statement on the inaction of the aristocratic class – the guardians of societal tradition – in the face of the third return of the tyrant Peisistratos and the uncertain future this event seemed to usher in. Ajax and Achilles play games as the Trojans storm the beached Greek ships – fiddling while Rome burned, if we can be allowed to mix our metaphors. According to Herodotus, the forces of the Athenian aristocrats were dining, napping, and throwing dice when Peisistratos landed with his troops and overtook them that day in 546 BC.[36] The mythological scene of the two heroes gaming thus symbolically represents an historical event – a model that many scholars would argue is common in Greek art.

But perhaps there is more here, not merely statement but social comment. In light of his earlier Herakles scenes, which can be interpreted as being complimentary to the new regime, Exekias has now – seemingly – switched allegiances, perhaps supporting the aristocratic faction for the stabilizing role it plays in Athenian society. Despite its many accomplishments, the third tyranny was born in violence brought by foreign troops (the Peisistratids fought with Argive mercenaries and allied forces from Eretria),[37]

and saw momentous changes and disruptions in conventional Athenian society. The process of enfranchisement of the non-aristocratic classes, decreased influence of the old aristocratic families, and increase in power of the new bureaucratic organs of the polis resulted in a radically different society, with ever increasing demands on individuals of all classes. Returning to the Boulogne amphora, it can be argued that the scene of Ajax's suicide can be read as a metaphor for these changes. An idea like this has already been suggested, in fact: in recent scholarship by the classicist Bernard Knox on the meaning of Ajax in Late Archaic and Early Classical literature.[38] Knox discusses Ajax as he appears in Sophocles, and describes him as a character representing reaction against the increasing demands of the democratic polis on its individual citizens.[39] Sophocles' Ajax is the story of that hero's resistance, as an independent nobleman and warrior, to the (somewhat arbitrary) authority of Agamemnon, primus inter pares as king of Mycenae, the most powerful of the Greek city-states during Homer's heroic age.

The Ajax of Sophocles is probably the earliest of that playwright's extant works, produced as early as 442 BC.[40] While the hero of the piece is depicted in a less than glamorous manner – maddened, as if seized by a furious daimon, he loses his senses and slaughters the Achaeans' livestock (fooled by Athena into thinking, however, that he had killed the Achaeans themselves) – Sophocles' goal seems nevertheless to juxtapose Ajax, as a symbol of defiant kingship, against the rule of law and polis as embodied by Menelaos and Agamemnon.[41] His final solution to the problem of honor that confronts him is a powerful statement in this regard, but in fact the conflict between these positions is played out afterward, as aggrieved parties debate over his corpse. After the hero's bloody suicide, Menelaos, the king of Sparta and member of the "council of

---

[33] Hurwit, p. 271–272.

[34] J. Hurwit, "Palm Trees and the Pathetic Fallacy in Archaic Greek Poetry and Art," CJ 77, 1982, p. 193–199; Fowler, cit. in note 4, p. 161; Hurwit 1985, p. 272 and n. 76.

[35] Hurwit 1985, p. 272.

[36] I. 63.

[37] I.61–I.62.

[38] Poet and Polis, in Backing into the Future: The Classical Tradition and Its Renewal, 1994, p. 191 ff. This essay originally appeared as the text of a lecture delivered for the Fondation Hardt in Geneva and was first published in the Entretiens XXIV, Sophocle.

[39] Ibidem, p. 191–193.

[40] J. Moore, Introduction to Ajax, The Complete Greek Tragedies, Vol. II: Sophocles, eds. D. Grene and R. Lattimore, 1992, p. 214.

[41] Knox, cit. in note 38, p. 201–202.

generals" that, ostensibly, governs the Greek forces at Troy, discovers Ajax's brother Teucer beside the body, and suggests to him that the Achaean generals will have their revenge on Ajax by denying him an honorable burial.[42] In his monologue, he argues that fear of law must be maintained, and that the Greek camp is simply a transposition of the state (polis), in military form (stratos), on foreign soil.[43] Lessers must obey their betters, or lack of discipline will breed anarchy and eventually the state will founder. Therefore, Ajax must be bound by rule of the council, even in death.

Agamemnon, king of Mycenae and supposed "leader" of the expedition against Troy, then appears and supports the arguments of his colleague by also invoking the rule of law and the legitimacy of the generals' council. This committee had commission to rule the Greeks in their cause against the Trojans – no royal prerogative, not even the size, strength, and valor of a great warrior like Ajax could exempt a man from this rule. Fighting at the forefront of the battle lines doesn't make a man of value, he argues – Agamemnon had done that, as had Menelaos, and Odysseus, and most all of the Greek warriors.[44] No, a man of value was one possessed of common sense, and one who submitted to the rule of law.[45] He expresses regret over the contest for Achilles' armor and how it turned out, but only in the sense that it provided an opportunity for Ajax to question the legitimacy of the generals' council.[46]

Teucer responds to both of these arguments with vigor. He states that Ajax had the status of an independent king and nobleman, not an underling.[47] This being the case, Teucer questions the rule of the council over Ajax in life or death – essentially placing aristocratic prerogative and the rights of the individual over the "democratic" rule of a committee, even a committee of powerful kings.[48] Ajax's motivation in the matter of Achilles' armor – and indeed the ultimate motivator of all of his actions on the plains of Troy – was aristocratic honor and fulfillment of

kingly oath, thus invoking the defining values of the warrior-elites of Dark Age and Archaic Greece.[49] Is he suggesting that Menelaos and Agamemnon are not possessed of such qualities, or that such qualities are alien to a government by collective?

Ajax's brother also attacks the very organs of the democratic process, a remarkable act when one considers that Sophocles lives in the radical democracy of mid-5th century Athens. He suggests to Menelaos that the vote over Achilles' armor had been fixed, and that he had suborned votes against Ajax by less than legitimate means.[50] Ironically, Ajax had always respected the voting process of the council, and had gladly accepted the combat assignments chosen by lot out of "…the crested helm…"[51] – he was thus betrayed by one of the defining elements of the democratic paradigm, and was correct in mistrusting its motives and doubting its validity. Sophocles has pitted, then, the rights of the noble against the power of the committee, and this conflict results in tragedy and loss.

Knox has argued that in the Ajax the claims of the polis are being advanced by "…unworthy spokesmen…" whose seemingly unreasonable claims and demands serve to "…enhance the dignity of that heroic corpse they wish to defile."[52] However, these demands – while perhaps presented in an extreme way by Menelaos and Agamemnon – would nevertheless have been familiar to the average Athenian citizen, who was exhorted by political leaders like Pericles to have "…a fanatical and irrational devotion to his city-state."[53] In the end, it is Ajax's defiance of the polis that results in his demise.[54] The old order must give

---

[42] Sophocles, Ajax 1067–1086.

[43] Knox, cit. in note 38, p. 202.

[44] Sophocles, Ajax 1226–1239.

[45] Ibidem, 1250–1254.

[46] Ibidem, 1239–1245.

[47] Ibidem, 1097–1110.

[48] Knox, cit. in note 38, p. 217–218.

---

[49] Sophocles, Ajax 1111–1114.

[50] Ibidem, e. 1135. Note that there were alternative traditions to the "vote" for Achilles' armor as seen in Sophocles. The Aithiopis and Little Iliad have the Greeks deciding based on the testimony of Trojan captives (C. Robert, Bild und Lied, 1881, p. 221; A. Severyns, Le cycle épique dans l'école d'Aristarque, 1928, p. 328–331), but before 500 BC the episode of the speeches and vote had developed, as is in evidence on a number of red figure cups executed by that time (Williams, cit. in note 12, p. 139–143).

[51] Sophocles, Ajax 1284–1287.

[52] Knox, cit. in note 38, p. 203–204.

[53] Thucydides II.43; Knox, cit. in note 38, p. 194 and 202–203. Thucydides has the Corinthians parrot this view, when they wonder about their Athenian adversaries who seem to always put the needs of their city first, even before their own lives (I.70).

way, but not without one final act of defiance – Ajax's actions bring into question the right of the polis, a mere human invention, to govern in all things.[55] The demise of traditional Archaic society will not be without mourners.[56]

Ajax's suicide then is not just the result of injured pride, but rather a final statement of aristocratic resolve against the rule of the mob – demokratia – even if it is a mob of kings and nobles, like that assembled at Troy. As supporting evidence for a work of Archaic art, some might argue that this view of Sophocles could be seen as anachronistic: he was of course a Classical author, living in a "full-blown" Athenian democracy several decades after Exekias. Not only that – he was an active participant in this democracy, holding positions as strategos, treasurer of the Delian League, and member of the council of the probouloi after the Sicilian disaster.[57] It is clear, however, that he was greatly sympathetic to the old ideals of the aristocracy, and aware of the dangers of the "Periclean ideal."[58] No less an authority than E.R. Dodds, in his 1957 masterpiece The Greeks and the Irrational called Sophocles "…the last great exponent of the Archaic world view."[59] Ajax was, in many ways, the very embodiment of this world view in both literature and art; it can be forcefully argued that Exekias' Boulogne amphora is yet another expression of this idea, with Ajax as its symbol.[60]

Thus, following Boardman's approach, we see that this may indeed be Exekias' Ajax, an Ajax who represents the Archaic ideals of the aristocracy in defiance of a tyrant who consolidates his power with popular support – increasing the power of the bureaucracy and polis at the expense of traditional governance structures and individual prerogatives. The inaction of this aristocracy, as symbolized in the Vatican Amphora, ultimately results in its demise. The suicide of Ajax is, in fact, the ultimate act of resistance, and an expression of the aristocratic mores that tyrants and mobs could never hope to realize. Thus, we have come full-circle, from the promise of a new order, to uncertainty and disillusionment, and finally to symbolic resistance which nevertheless is doomed to failure. Not long after the end of Exekias' career as a vase painter, the Athens that he had known – its government, society, and artistic and cultural life – would change irrevocably.

---

[54] Knox, cit. in note 38, p. 201

[55] Ibidem, p. 217–218.

[56] Sophocles is not the only poet who has been ascribed such motives. Pindar – who is traditionally described as a "mouthpiece" of the weakened aristocracy of the Early Classic period – dealt with the theme of Ajax's shame and suicide in several of his famous odes (Nemean VII.23–27 and VII.21–27; Isthmian IV.52–57). He casts Odysseus and the general council as the villains – they are jealous of the prowess of noble Ajax and conspire against him in "secret ballots." Thus, the organs of democracy are again seen in a negative light in the Ajax story.

[57] Knox, cit. in note 38, p. 195.

[58] Ibidem, p. 218.

[59] See p. 49; Dodds also reminds us that the Archaic period as an *intellectual* era does not really end in Athens until the development of the Sophistic movement; thus Sophocles, and Pindar, for that matter, are truly "Archaic" poets (p. 50, n. 1).

[60] This final connection between literature and vase painting has been explored in a number of sources. Fowler sees Exekias' depiction of Ajax's suicide – as well as other painted scenes such as those on the Vatican amphora – as indicative of that artist's embodiment of the Archaic "aesthetic" and his understanding of juxtaposition as used in Archaic poetry (p. 161). Indeed, in comparing Exekias' suicide of Ajax with Pindar's descriptions of the same event, Fowler, cit. in note 5, suggests that Exekias "…anticipates Pindar…" by creating a scene in which Ajax is somehow vindicated through his (implied) actions (p. 163). Hurwit's attempts to show connections between art and other aspects of Greek culture are probably the most well-known, however. He has argued that Exekias' remarkable sensibility and revolutionary style – in which he is able to convey anticipation and emotion, as on the Boulogne amphora – may suggest that the artist was familiar with the development of early tragedy, and may have seen a play which dealt with the suicide of Ajax (1985, p. 272).

**Fig. 1.** Black-figure amphora by Exekias, Musei Vaticani, photo after Albizzati, Vasi Antichi Dipinti del Vaticano.

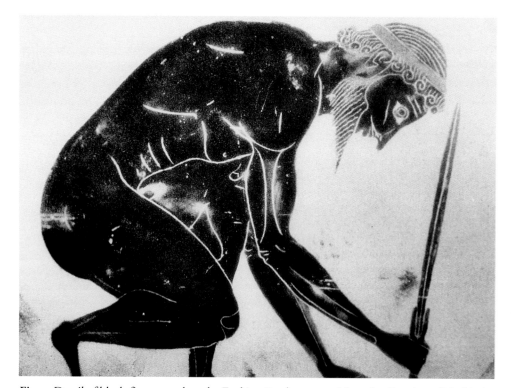

**Fig. 2.** Detail of black-figure amphora by Exekias, Boulogne-sur-Mer, after Buschor, Griechische Vasen.

# MORTAL AND DIVINE PERFORMANCES: NEW EVIDENCE FROM THE BREAKERS

*Susan Heuck Allen*

I would like to thank my former professor, Ross Holloway, for his continued guidance and support, and to acknowledge the late Tony Hackens for arranging access to Archaic Greek temple sites of Kerkyra in 1985. I am further indebted to my late esteemed professor, Cedric Boulter, for an inspired introduction to Attic vase painting, and to Dietrich von Bothmer for a follow-up session at the Metropolitan Museum of Art.

During a 1990 A.I.A. tour of The Breakers, the Newport, Rhode Island summer home of railroad and steamship magnate Cornelius Vanderbilt II,[1] a guide described several vases, displayed in lunettes above the bookcases in the library, as modern reproductions.[2] Subsequently, Martha Joukowsky, then President of the Archaeological Institute of America, alerted me to the vases and asked me to look at them.[3] Until my visit in January 1991, these vessels had not been professionally examined and were assumed to be good nineteenth-century reproductions, selected as furnishings for the interior of Vanderbilt's Newport "cottage". After examining all of the pieces closely for repairs, restorations, and overpainting, I determined that, rather than eight good reproductions, the Vanderbilts' library

possessed authentic ancient vases from the late sixth to the end of the fourth century B.C.[4] This article focuses on the decoration on two unpublished Attic black-figured neck amphorae in the collection which are related by their iconography. Both bear depictions of musical performances, one mortal, the other divine. L.176 preserves scenes of a kithara competition, probably at the mousikoi agones of the Panathenaic Festival, L.178 shows a hero's performance.

## L. 176. [Fig. 1 and 2]

Attic black-figured neck amphora
H: 43.9 cm. Rim D: 20.0 cm. Foot D: 14.68 cm.
Broken and restored. Considerable over-painting.

*The interior of the echinus mouth and neck is fully glazed. Reserved at the top, the rim is black with a reserved band beneath the lip followed by a black band. On the neck there is a circumscribed lotus-palmette chain comprised of five lotuses and four palmettes on which there are five leaves up and five down. Reserved bands separate this from the raised fillet with added red at the junction of neck and shoulder and from the carefully circumscribed red and black tongue pattern on the shoulder. On the body beneath the picture plane there is a ground line on which the figures stand. Beneath this are double black bands above and below a chain of circled upright lotus buds with dots in the interstices below. Between this and the foot are rays. The torus foot is black with the lower part*

---

[1] It remained a private residence from 1895 to 1948. In 1972 the Preservation Society of Newport County purchased it. Although the purchase records have not yet been located, the vases were inventoried after the death of Cornelius Vanderbilt II and again when the property was transferred to the society in 1963. By 1972 most of the antiquities collection had been sold by the grandchildren. These vases represent only a fraction of the original inventory of antiquities in the house. From a cursory perusal of labels attached to the bases of several pieces, Dietrich von Bothmer has suggested that they originated in Italy from a ducal sale of the 1890's.

[2] I would like to thank the late Countess Anthony Szàpàry, granddaughter of Cornelius Vanderbilt II, for her permission to publish them. See John Tschirch's letter to the author, March 4, 1991. I would also like to thank Armin Allen for having the vases photographed for publication in this article.

[3] Letter to the author of October 3, 1990.

[4] The vases are from a private collection, Newport, RI – presently on view at The Breakers. These findings were presented as a paper at the 1992 AIA annual meeting in New Orleans, an abstract of which was published. Susan Heuck Allen, Mortal and Divine Performances: New Evidence at The Breakers, American Journal of Archaeology 93/2, 1993, pp. 329–330. I would like to thank Alan L. Boegehold and John H. Oakley for commenting on an earlier version of this manuscript.

*reserved. The triple-reeded handles are glazed on the upper and outer surfaces and reserved beneath. Below each are four palmettes and three lotuses with a dot at the center. Palmettes on the obverse have six leaves while the right palmettes on the reverse have seven leaves, the left, six.*

On Side A a bearded kitharode, standing tall with rigid posture, mounts the high bema[5] for a contest [Fig. 1].[6] His right leg bends with the weight of the heavy instrument while his left leg remains on the ground. A red sash or strap helps steady the instrument which he cradles with his left arm. Judging from the position of his hands and fingers, he has perhaps just caught the attention of his audience with a strum across the seven strings. Several details point to the elevated status of the performer. A red fillet confines his long hair which is rolled up in a sort of pageboy cut while his beard is neat and well-trimmed. Although barefoot, he wears a long white himation with crenellated edge over a black chiton. His kithara is equally elaborate with the details of its inner arms and the lower edge of the sounding box ornamented, perhaps with ivory as was Apollo's phorminx elaphantodetos.[7] As is common, he stands between two bearded men, listeners or judges, who lean on knotty staves.[8] They wear ornamented himatia and those who stand have wreaths of long, straight branches bound round their heads which suggest a difference in status.[9] Seated listeners wear red fillets in their hair like the contestants.[10]

Side B [Fig. 2] also depicts a mature kitharoidos stepping up to the bema. Like most performers, he stands to play, holding the instrument upright or tipped slightly away from him, with his left wrist in the sling and left fingers curved as if damping the strings. Presumably the thumb is bent over in front of the palm (as on Side A). With his right hand he holds the plektron out beyond the strings, at the outer edge of the soundbox, giving the impression that he too has just finished an outward sweep across the strings.[11]

Similar scenes on obverse and reverse are characteristic of a phase in the late sixth century. Yet these scenes are not strictly identical. The performers are different individuals with varied renderings of facial details: the one on Side B wears a mustache whereas the one on Side A does not. Audience members also differ. On Side A the seated gentleman is bearded and leans forward, listening to the contestant with rapt attention. On Side B, however, the seated figure, marred by restoration, is an unbearded youth who turns away, perhaps an affected Athenian dandy[12] who inhales a fragrant flower while enjoying musical performances, or, distracted and looking past the decorative lotus bud toward the scene on the obverse, perhaps a humorous commentary on the quality of performance of the contestant on Side B.[13] If this is the case, the paired performances could be taking place simultaneously as part of the same contest.[14] Shapiro has suggested that such pairings of musical scenes consonant with Panathenaic iconography give a taste of the festival.[15] The two kithar-

---

[5] On both sides of L. 176 the bema is high and boxy and has one incised horizontal division. In general, great variation exists – from a high, simple box to low and wide, from a box with one or two horizontal incised divisions, to a stepped platform with one to three shallow steps, reflecting the fact that it was probably a temporary structure, made of wood, set up just for the Panathenaia in the center of the Agora and that its shape was not nearly as important as the performances which took place upon it.

[6] Shapiro finds this posture common to the earliest depictions of Panathenaic kithara players. H.A. Shapiro, Mousikoi Agones: Music and Poetry at the Panathenaia, in J. Neils, ed., Goddess and Polis: The Panathenaic Festival in Ancient Athens, 1992, p. 67.

[7] Aristophanes, Birds, 219. The Homeric word, phorminx, reserved for Apollo's instrument, is also used by Theokritos to describe the instrument on which Herakles was instructed (Herakliskos 24.110).

[8] Shapiro suggests that the association of knotty sticks with bearded men denotes judges (Shapiro, cit. in note 6, p.60) or forked staves. Ibidem, p. 74. Elsewhere, Shapiro takes the standing figures to be audience members and the seated ones, judges. Shapiro, Art and Cult under the Tyrants in Athens, 1989, pp. 43, 62. Paris F82–3 shows listening judges, one seated: M. Maas and J.M. Snyder, Stringed Instruments of Ancient Greece, 1989, p. 61. Leningrad 17295 (ibidem, fig. 10).

[9] Maas and Snyder , cit. in note 9, p. 61. London 1926.6–28.7, CVA BM4, UK5, pl.61: 4a and b; Kassel pelike T 675, Shapiro, cit. in note 6, fig. 47; Oldenburg Stadtmuseum, ibidem, pl.22a.

[10] A White Ground lekythos by the Athena Painter shows the hieropoioi, a board of eight magistrates in charge of the Panathenaia, identified by inscriptions. They are draped in himatia and have red fillets and branches bound round their heads. J. Neils, The Panathenaia: An Introduction, in Neils, cit. in note 6, pp.18, 183, cat. no 55, ABV 522,34). Perhaps the witnesses on L. 176 could be hieropoioi.

[11] Maas and Snyder, cit. in note 8, p. 34.

odes, perhaps performing in the same contest since they are united by the turning figure, give a heightened sense of competition.

On both sides the artist has chosen to include vegetation in the form of a high-arching, stylized vine, a common filler element on vases of this period. This branching in the field and lack of incision in the lotus-palmette chain on the neck characterize works by Beazley's Leagros Group. As such, L. 176 would date to the late sixth century (ca. 520–510 B.C.). Various stylistic details suggest that it is the work of the Acheloos Painter.[16] These include the use of the lithe vines with no point of origin;[17] large chunky figures which fill the zone; details such as the in-

cision on the eye, ear, and mustache; knobby noses, jutting jaws and painted beards. The concentric circular ear is seen here and on the Hermes on the painter's name vase in Berlin.[18] His other ear style, with a deep, pendant loop for a lobe, is also seen on this vase. In general, his work is characterized by long, bulbous noses; incised simple arc eye brows; eyes consisting of triangles on either side of concentric incised pupils and irises; incised pursed, projecting lips; incised mustaches composed of parallel lines, and beards with added red and edged with incised parallel lines. Moreover, both the composition, closed by a twisted figure at each side of the picture or one facing inwards,[19] and the idea of replicating one scene on both sides of the vase are common to this painter.[20] Likewise characteristic of the Acheloos Painter are the crenellated himation[21] on both kitharodes and twigs bound round the heads of the listeners.[22] Most telling of all, however, is his humorous depiction of the scenes:[23] the distracted figure who looks away from one performance to another, and the conceits, namely, figures such as sirens and birds perched on decorative palmettes.[24] Here, the seated figures rest not on the usual folding stool, or okladias, but rather on the decorative side palmettes.[25]

In the mousikoi agones of the Panathenaic Festival in Athens, there were several contests[26] with the most prestigious competitions held for kitharodes who sang while accompanying themselves and kitharists who played.[27] The depiction of their performances on vases[28] became popular in the second half of the sixth century during the rule of the tyrant Peisistratos and his sons.[29] The kitharodes

[12] R.R. Holloway, Music at the Panathenaic Festival, Archaeology 71, 1966, pp.112–119. See ABV 370, 134 and ABV 270. (ABV=J.D. Beazley, Attic Black-Figure Vase Painters, 1956).The Princeton Painter's NY 1989.281.89 shows bearded audience members sniffing flowers on the reverse (D. von Bothmer, Notes on the Princeton Painter, Antike Kunst 30, 1987, pp. 64–65, pl. 9:1–2). See also K. Schauenburg, Eine neue Amphora des Andokidesmalers, Jahrbuch des Deutschen Archäologischen Instituts 76, 1961, 50, fig.2; Basel BS491; Louvre G1, ARV² 3,2. Shapiro, cit. in note 8, p.42 and Shapiro, cit. in note 6, p. 62. (ARV²=J.D. Beazley, Attic Red-figure Vase-painters, 2nd edition, Oxford 1963).

[13] For jokes at the expense of competing kithara players, see Pherekrates fr.6 (Edmonds).

[14] For vases where two musical scenes are joined in a continuous frieze, see Harvard 1977.216.2397, Shapiro, cit. in note 6, pp. 70–71, n. 112, figs.49 a and b. NY 07.286.72 shows a kithara player on side A and an aulode on side B. Ibidem, pp. 52, 71, 156, cat. no 19. A later red-figured calyx krater by the Painter of Munich 2335 shows four events (two musical and two athletic). Larisa 86/101, ibidem, p. 61, fig. 39a,b.

[15] For two Panathenaic kithara competitions, see Toronto 919.25.2. CVA I, II, pls. 15: 1, 16. Here kitharodes stand on both sides of the vessel between two Doric columns surmounted by cocks, but there is no unifying subject matter that brings both sides together such as can be seen on L.176. See also K. Schauenburg Herakles Mousikos, Jahrbuch des Deutschen Archäologischen Instituts 32, p. 66, note 70). Shapiro, cit. in note 9, pp.41–42, Shapiro, cit. in, note 6, pp. 60–61, n.59, pp. 70–71.200, 202. For a musical scene on one side combined with a possible performance on the other, see Group E: San Antonio 86.134.40, ibidem, p. 65, cat. no. 20.

[16] The artist was first mentioned by J.D. Beazley in Attic Black-Figured Vases: A Sketch, Proceedings of the British Academy 14, 1928, p.46, appendix VII. The latest study of his work is that of E. Moignard, The Acheloos Painter and Relations, Annual of the British School at Athens 77, 1982, pp.201–211.

[17] In scene with rhapsode, Dunedin E 48.226, ABV 386, 12; with aulode, Basel BS 06.294, ABV 384, 16; name vase in Berlin 1851, ABV 383, 3, ABV 383, 4; London B 167, ABV 382,1; MMA NY 49.11.1, ABV 384, 19; Fitzwilliam GR 125, 1864; Fitzwilliam GR 51, 1937, ABV 340, 1; Basel MM 56, 77; or Toledo 58.69; and Smithsonian 1979.696.01, ABV 386, 9, Neils, cit. in note 6, p. 164, cat. no.30.

[18] Berlin 1851, ABV 383, 3, and Smithsonian 1979.696.01, ABV 386, 9, Neils, cit. in note 6, p.164, cat. no.30.

[19] These twisted poses, with the viewer turning to look behind (Smithsonian 1979.696.01, ABV 386, 9) and the animated gestures of the milling audience members recall the painter's contemporaries in red figure, the Pioneers.

[20] Toledo 58.69A; Munich 1549, ABV 383, 12; Berlin 1845; and Wurzburg 210, ABV 373, 178. For the same subject with slightly different treatment, see Smithsonian 1979.696.01, ABV 386, 9.

were depicted as mature professionals whose status was often signified by their regalia.[30] Indeed most kitharodes on

vases are shown in richly ornamented chitons and himatia,[31] recalling those of Apollo, the divine kitharist par excellence.[32] Successful performers are also crowned sometimes (although neither is on the vase under discussion here).[33]

---

[21] The closest parallel for the crenellated himation is on an amphora by the Acheloos Painter in Basel BS 06.294, ABV 384, 16. Another example, kindly brought to my attention by Dietrich von Bothmer, is Roš (ex Mikas 1954; ex Péreire), ABV 386, 6. These crenellated patterns are sometimes found on the himation of Apollo kitharoidos London B260 and the Swing Painter's Leningrad 1494, ABV 309, 85 and London B139, ABV 139,12. Crenellated patterns in himatia and other garments such as Thracian mantles are not unusual. They can be found in various renditions in the work of Group E (on Apollo kitharoidos: Boston CVA 1, 3–4, pl.5; Thracian mantle: Oxford 1965.135, D. von Bothmer, *The Amasis Painter and his World*, 1987, 132, fig. 80); the Swing Painter (aulete: Orvieto faina 52, E. Böhr, *Der Schaukelmaler*, 1982, pl.7; Naples 81305, ibidem, pl.81; on Apollo kitharoidos: Leningrad 1494, ibidem, pl.100; on Athena's peplos: Compiègne 981, ibidem, pl.94; on Athena's himation: Munich 1489, ibidem, pls.109, 110; elder: Rome (Market), ibidem, pl.3, Erlangen M245, ibidem, pl.52; Thracian mantle: San Simeon 5476, Berlin Pergamon Museum, ibidem, pl.45, Würzburg L 186, ibidem, pl.95; Tarquinia RC 1871, ibidem, pl.153; himation: Munich 1395, ibidem, pl.34; charioteer's selvage: NY 17.230.8, ibidem, pls.77, 78; on garment: Eleusis 275, ibidem, pl.90. The Antimenes Painter (Thracian mantle on Dionysos) Zürich ETH 8, J. Bürow, *Der Antimenesmaler*, 1989, pl.5, (Thracian mantle: Munich 1548, Würzburg L 186, ibidem, pl.95; Tarquinia RC 1871, ibidem, pl.153; and the workshop of the Antimenes Painter (Thracian mantle on Dionysos) Zürich 2467, CVA 1 pl.14. Euphronios also used the motif for a Thracian mantle (Munich 2620 ARV2 16, 17) as well as in the painter's white ground work (Paris Bib. Nat. II 474, pl.22.814). It occurs on the himation of a satyr carrying Hermes' caduceus on a psykter by Douris (London E768) and on the himation of an aulete on the exterior of a kylix in Dresden (33), in Brygos's work on the Würzburg kylix (E. Pfuhl, *Malerei und Zeichnung*, 1923, 138: #419 and 139: #420), Nausikaa Painter on Orpheus kitharoidos: (ibidem, 194, #511 JHS 25 pl.1, 530), and ibidem, 217 #554, as well as on shrouds: (ibidem, 216, #553). In Euboean Black Figure: NY 06.1021.35 and Fogg 2271, D. von Bothmer, Euboean Black Figure in New York, Metropolitan Museum Journal 2, 1969 29, figs 2 and 4. Von Bothmer suggests that the pattern may have been inspired by the pteryges of a linen corselet/cuirass (Swing Painter, Böhr op.cit., pls. 60, 91).

[22] For this headgear with the Acheloos Painter, see London B 167, ABV 382,1; Fitzwilliam GR 51, 1937, near the Acheloos Painter-Para 169, 8bis; Roš (ex Mikas 1954; ex Péreire), ABV 386, 6). (J.D.Beazley Paralipomena, Oxford 1971=Para). See also note 8.

[23] Beazley (cit. in note 16, p.46) describes his "satyrical style," and his "comic vein" in J.D. Beazley *The Development of Black Figure*, Berkeley 1951, p.86. See Dunedin E 48.226, ABV 386, 12.

---

[24] See the siren on Rome ABV 383, 4 and the bird on Berlin 1851, ABV 383, 3. I thank Dietrich von Bothmer for bringing these to my attention.

[25] Both this conceit and that of the crenellated himation point to a possible relationship between the Acheloos Painter and his predecessors, Swing Painter who used both and the Princeton Painter. For a siren on a spiral by the Swing Painter, see Leningrad 1494, (Böhr, cit. in note 21, no. 98, pl.100). This figure, turned to the outside, twists its head back to center to witness the action. One of the first occurrences of this is seen in the work of the Princeton Painter where sirens can be found perched on spiral palmette tendrils. See von Bothmer, cit. in note 12, pl. 7. Also see cocks turning away from central action in the work of the Princeton Painter NY 1989.281.89, Neils, cit. in note 6, p. 43, 155, cat. no. 18.

[26] However, the very presence of musical competitions at the Panathenaia has recently been questioned by J. Pollitt, The Visual Impact of the Panathenaia on Classical Greek Art, in Neils, cit. in note 6.

[27] The inscription giving prize information dates to the first half of the fourth century B.C. (J.A. Davison, Notes on the Panathenaia, Journal of Hellenic Studies 78, 1958, p.42; Aristotle. Ath Pol. 60.3; IG ii–iii² 2311).

[28] It is not always possible to tell which performers are kitharodes and which simply play their instruments. (For instance Apollo and Herakles are never shown with their mouths open as if in song.) In the earliest images of Panathenaic performances, the kithara player's pose is stiff, certainly less animated than in later Archaic scenes where the kitharode is sometimes shown singing with his head thrown back and mouth open. (These are all later than L. 176: Kassel pelike T.675, Shapiro, cit. in note 6, fig.47; Brygos Painter, Boston 26.61; Berlin Painter NY 56.171.38.) Usually in the early scenes the musician is standing on or only just mounting the platform or bema, and the performance has not yet begun. In these cases it is impossible to tell which type of artist is being represented.

[29] The first certain image of a Panathenaic kitharode or kitharist dates to around 530 B.C. Representations of the kithara are more common on Black Figure than Red Figure and the frequency of the kithara to other instruments is much higher for Black Figure though it falls off dramatically among those made after 500 B.C. when there is a widespread change in iconography (Maas and Snyder, cit. in note 8, p. 55). Political grounds for this seem clear. (See below.) Events heavily sponsored by the tyrants would seem to have fallen out of fashion after their demise.

Vines are often shown in scenes thought to represent Panathenaic competitions[34] which are assumed to have been held outdoors in the center of the Agora prior to the building of the Odeion by Perikles.[35] Although the scenes on L.176 need not represent events from the Panathenaia and the shape of the vase is not Panathenaic, numerous details support a Panathenaic connection: the bema, the presence of judges with fillets or branches bound round their heads, the elegance of the kitharodes' garments, and the pairing of scenes on the obverse and reverse as if depicting dueling kitharodes. Since kithara contests were instituted during the late sixth century when Peisistratos and his sons were in control and since it has been established further that Peisistratos and Hipparchos were supporters of public performances in the City Dionysia and on Delos,[36] one can infer Peisistratid backing for the mousikoi agones of the Greater Panathenaia in general.

Thus the iconography of the kitharodes' performance at the games can be said to be Peisistratan in theme, reflecting the prestige and glamor of such performances under the tyrants. I would like to suggest further that the Acheloos Painter, like the Lysippides Painter[37] and the Priam Painter,[38] was much affected by his times and chose to produce vases with innovative subject matter reflecting the preferences of the tyrants. He frequently portrayed Herakles, the Peisistratid hero, in unconventional episodes,[39] as well as fountain houses (new public works projects?), and musical performances connected with Peisistratid festivals and contemporary poets.[40]

## L. 178. [Fig. 3 and 4]

Attic black-figured neck amphora

H: 42.2 cm. Rim D: 19.20 cm. Foot D: 14.128 cm. Broken and mended. Foot restored. Considerable overpainting. Some chips were once restored in plaster.

*The interior of the echinus mouth and neck is fully glazed. Reserved at the top, the rim is black with a reserved band beneath the lip followed by a black band. On the neck there is an incised circumscribed lotus-palmette chain comprising five lotuses and four palmettes on which there are five leaves up*

[30] In Herodotus (1.24) the legendary kitharode, Arion, asks to perform for captain and crew, who will surely kill him otherwise, before he casts himself into the sea. Prior to performing, he dons his elaborate robes, mentioned four times in the passage. He even wears them when he dives into the sea fully accoutred though the long, flowing robes would certainly have dragged him down.

[31] The elegant himatia are gathered at the shoulder with brooches. The Greek preserves this connection with porpe for brooch, hence the name epiporpama (Pl. Com fr. 10 Edmonds, vol I., p.492).

[32] Maas and Snyder, cit. in note 8, pp. 54, 58. However, unlike the youthful Apollo, mortal kitharodes are shown as mature, bearded men, as on the vase discussed here.

[33] See London 1926.6–28.7, (note 9). IG ii–iiie 2311 mentions the crowns and prize money given to winners at the Panathenaia.

[34] For instance, Dunedin E48.226 (ABV 386, 12), shows a rhapsodic competition held outdoors. In some examples the kithara player stands between two columns surmounted by cocks, almost certainly meant to connote a Panathenaic context, London B 139, ABV 139, 12; San Antonio 86.134.40, Neils, cit. in note 6, cat. no. 20 (unbearded, perhaps a kitharistes); Toronto 919.25.2, Maas and Snyder, cit. in note 8, p. 61.

[35] Post holes in the middle of the open Agora may indicate the presence of temporary wooden bleachers. (J. Neils, The Panathenaia: An Introduction, in Neils, cit. in note 6, p. 18; H.A. Thompson and R.E. Wycherley, The Athenian Agora XIV: The Agora of Athens, 1972, pp.126–129). Shapiro, cit. in note 6, p. 44; R.E. Wycherley The Stones of Athens, 1979, pp. 215–216, n.21, Davison, cit. in note 27, pp. 33–36; Plutarch Pericles 13.5–6.

[36] Shapiro, cit. in note 8, p. 42, notes 205, 206 and in Shapiro, Hipparchos and the Rhapsodes, in L. Kurke and C. Dougherty, eds., Cultural Poetics in Ancient Greece, 1993.

[37] J. Boardman, Herakles, Peisistratos and Eleusis, Journal of Hellenic Studies, 95, 1975, pp. 11–12.

[38] J. Boardman, Herakles, Peisistratos and Sons, Revue Archeologique, 1972, p. 64.

[39] See note 70 below.

[40] See Vatican 417, ABV 384, 26; NY 56.171.22, ABV 383,9; Louvre F 272, ABV 383, 6; and London B 167, ABV 382, 1. Boardman has argued that the changes in the canonical treatment of certain Herakles stories and the introduction of new ones occurred during the time of Peisistratos; e.g., the new-style Kerberos scenes, new vignettes of Herakles throwing the lion or lying with it, Herakles the kitharist, Herakles at the feast with Athena, Herakles driving the bull to sacrifice. Boardman goes further to suggest that these may be in part due to their treatment in lost works by Stesichoros (cit. in note 37, p.10). See also W. Burkert, The Making of Homer in the 6th Century B.C.: Rhapsodes versus Stesichoros, in von Bothmer, cit. in note 12, p.51. For the well-documented impact of his poetry on Attic art through the medium of kitharodic performances, see M. Robertson, Geryoneis: Stesichoros and the Vase-Painters, Classical Quarterly 19, 1969, pp.207–221 and Shapiro, cit. in note 9. See notes 76 and 77 below.

*and five down and added red. Reserved bands separate this from the raised fillet with added red at the junction between neck and shoulder and from the hastily circumscribed black tongue pattern on the shoulder. On the body beneath the picture plane there is a ground line on which the figures stand. Beneath this are double black bands above and below a maeander which proceeds to the left. Below this is a chain of circled upright lotus buds with dots in the interstices below. Beneath this, between another double black band and the foot, are rays. The torus foot is black with the lower part restored. The triple-reeded handles are glazed on the top and exterior surfaces and reserved beneath. Below each of them are four palmettes and three lotuses with a cross at the center. The palmettes have five leaves.*

L.178 also dates stylistically to the late sixth century. In shape and proportion it is similar to the amphora just discussed. The subject matter of the latter was most likely inspired by or based on the conventions of the former, but the scene on side A of L.178 is much rarer since, rather than depicting a mortal kitharode or even Apollo (his divine archetype), it shows the hero Herakles stepping up to a bema to serenade Athena and Dionysos with his kithara [Fig. 3]. Side B depicts a frontal horse and rider between two armed warriors with their hounds [Fig. 4].

Herakles is a monumental figure like the seated gods Athena and Dionysos who, if they stood erect, would burst through the tongue pattern of the shoulder. The hero hunches over as he mounts the bema to play,[41] and, to accommodate the large figure, the painter has also shortened the boxy bema. Like his mortal counterparts on L. 176, Herakles stands, holding the instrument tipped slightly away, having caught the attention of his divine audience before beginning his concert. Rather than the customary long robes of the performer, Herakles wears his trademark lion skin and a chitoniskos, and is armed with his characteristic quiver, bow, and sword.[42] The bearded figure has incisions articulating facial features, fingers,

toes, kneecap[43] and musculature.[44] Hasty incisions mark internal divisions in the sleeve, skin and its pelt pattern.[45] The lion's head subtly echoes that of Herakles. His kithara is no less elaborate than those on L. 176 or Apollo's, with substantial parts of the inner arms and lower edge of the sounding box rendered in added white to simulate ivory.[46]

On the right, an armed and rigid-postured Athena[47] sits facing center on an okladias, or folding stool.[48] With her right hand she beckons him to proceed, while she holds a spear in her left. The goddess is dressed in a dotted chiton, himation, aegis, and Attic helmet.[49] There is considerable use of added red and white to complement the incised details of her garb and weapon.[50] Two incised arcs mark flesh folds at the base of her neck and the profile of her forelock.

---

[41] When he is shown on the bema, he is almost always depicted as stepping up to it. The exceptions are Boulogne 78 (ABV 277, 17) and Tarquinia 681, CVA 1, pl.12 where he stands to the side of it before mounting and Worcester where he stands on top of it. Schauenburg, cit. in note 15.

[42] Shapiro has discussed the difficulty of distinguishing mortal Athenian kithara players from their divine role-model, Apollo (cit. in note 6, p. 65). Thanks to his familiar costume and accoutrements this is not a problem here.

[43] See NY 56.171.14 in the Manner of the Lysippides Painter and NY 58.32.

[44] See the Hermes on Toronto 919.5.141 in the Manner of the Lysippides Painter.

[45] NY 58.32 and from the Group of Munich 1501 and the Painter of London B 272: Louvre F243, CVA pl.48: 1, 4, 7.

[46] As in the case of the first vase, this may simulate Apollo's phorminx elaphantodetos. See above, note 6.

[47] Athena is always depicted as armed in the Herakles Kitharoidos scenes. See below. This may have to do with the new cult of Athena Promachos in Athens during the time of the tyrants as well as her armed aspect in the story of the Gigantomachy where she fought alongside Herakles so as to insure the gods' success. Boardman asserts that this could explain why he was later accepted as a god and that Dionysos' similarly special role in the fight made him another special protégé of sixth century Athens. J. Boardman, Image and Politics in Sixth Century Athens, in Ancient Greek and Related Pottery Proceedings of the International Vase Symposium, Amsterdam 1984, H.A.G. Brijder, ed., 1985, p.243. Dionysos and Herakles are also shown feasting together (as if at a mortal symposium) in another innovative image from Peisistratid times. Ibidem, p. 244.

[48] This would be appropriate temporary seating for audience members and judges in scenes from musical contests at the Panathenaia.

[49] For design and similar intrusion into the area of the tongue pattern, see Toronto 919.5.141.

[50] Added red is on helmet, aegis, spear, chiton and himation. Her flesh is unfortunately grossly overpainted.

On the left a stiff Dionysos sits on an okladias,[51] his static body passively awaiting the performance.[52] He raises a kantharos high with his left hand as if to offer a toast to the performer. In his right hand he holds a forked vine which branches out behind the figures. Consistent with his character, he wears his hair long with luxuriant curls trailing down his back, and on his head he wears a wreath of ivy leaves. Bearded and mature, he is dressed in an elaborate red-striped chiton and red dotted himation with white dotted crosses.[53] Hasty incisions clarify the lines of drapery around his neck, chest, arms, knees, the kantharos and vine in his grasp as well as his beard, curls, eye, and lips.[54]

The reverse depicts a frontal horse and naked rider flanked by two hoplites and their hounds [Figure 4]. The rider's head, turned to his right, and the angle of his right arm balance the horse's head which turns to its left. The rider's left arm is not shown and his legs dangle asymmetrically. He wears a red fillet on his head and carries two spears. His ear is rendered by incised concentric circles, while incisions also delineate his closely cropped hair, facial features, elbows, kneecaps and musculature. The horse's head, shown in profile, is rendered with incisions and added red for the upright incised mane. There are two parallel lines for the brow, a long vertical tear duct, and generous jaw. Ornamented with hanging red and white decorations, the red breast band runs horizontally across the horse's breast and obscures the contours of the upper chest. This area is articulated with two close parallel lines which terminate at the shoulders, further indicated by incised arcs.[55] The tail is hastily detailed with a vertical zigzag incision while the rendering of ankles and hooves is boxy.

The hoplites stand in profile facing the center. They wear helmets and greaves[56] and carry two spears and shields. The figure on the right wears a Corinthian helmet and carries a shield with an unusual shield device, a ketos or sea monster.[57] The figure on the left walks to the left, but turns his head abruptly to the right so as to face the center. He wears a Boeotian helmet and himation and carries a shield decorated with a bearded serpent.[58] Their hounds are elegantly drawn with sketchily incised details portraying the chest by a wide arc, facial details and ruff, as well as two parallel lines marking the haunches and the incised contour of the tails.

Considering the chronological stylistic criteria of sufficiently attenuated and incised palmette-lotus chain with added red on the neck and the monochrome tongue pattern below, the vase appears to date earlier in the sixth century (ca. 530–520 B.C.) than L. 176. Boardman has suggested that the Lysippides Painter may have invented the scene of Herakles Kitharoidos.[59] He certainly painted our earliest renditions of it.[60] That it was a favorite of his and the later Acheloos Painter can be seen from the number of their vases devoted to the scene.[61] There are numerous affinities which L. 178 shares with the work of the Lysippides Painter such as the iconography on Side A, the treatment of the greaves on the reverse, branching in the

---

[51] Both his and Athena's stools are decorated with added red and white.

[52] A close parallel for the static Dionysos is on Howard-Sneed 1985, ex Pizzati, ABV 370, 134.

[53] For the same design on the garments, see Cleveland 27.433 and Toronto 919.5.141.

[54] Added red is used for his beard, vine leaf wreath and ornately decorated drapery. Added red further ornaments his himation.

[55] One of these is almost obscured by overpainting which may also have concealed the second area over the shoulder joint and the characteristic arcs of the upper chest.

[56] These are decorated with added red, one line on the exterior and a spiral on the interior and two incised lines on the bottom. See parallels below, footnote 62.

[57] This has unfortunately been obscured by the overpainting. For parallels, see Seltman pl.38:11; *Group E*: once in Baden, Roš, ABV 133, 5; Stesias kalos Berlin 1698, ABV 136, 54; *Antimenes Painter*: Munich 1548 (ABV 273, 11, Bürow, cit. in note 21, pl.78); Erlangen I 1196, 2 (unpublished); Port Sunlight 5015, ex Hope 21 (M. Robertson Greek, Etruscan and Roman Vases in the Lady Lever Art Gallery, Port Sunlight Liverpool, 1987) 25–26, pls 13 a, b, 14, cat. no 14; Dublin National Museum 1921–93; Rome American Academy ph. R.I. 63.1623; *Syleus Painter*: Louvre Cp 1103, ABV 251, 37; NY Market Royal Athena column krater HAR 01; *Group of Munich 1501 and the Painter of London B272*: Orvieto ABV 391, bottom no.3, Para 153 no.8; *Douris*: Baltimore-Johns Hopkins ARV² 442, no.215.

[58] Both devices are executed in added white while the bands around the circumference of the shields are rendered in added red. Both devices are seen in the work of the Antimenes Painter; e.g., the bearded serpent on Baltimore 48.17 (Bürow, cit. in note 21, pl.48) and ketos on Munich 1548 (ibidem, pl.78).

[59] Boardman, cit. in note 38, pp. 10–11.

field, and the frontal horseman – all of which are equally at home in the repertory of both the Antimenes Painter and the Lysippides Painter. Yet the iconography and stylistic details seem to point to a different artist. The Group of Munich 1501/ the Painter of London B 272 observes strict symmetry and strong centrality in the scenes of frontal horseman and flanking hoplites, the conceit of one figure turning back on the central composition, and irregularity of placement of side palmettes. Details seen in L. 178, such as the incision of the knee cap, the closely cropped hair of the rider, the dangling legs of the rider, incised lines to indicate the back leg muscles of the hoplites, the double incised lines at the base of the hoplites' greaves, the form and incised details on the hounds, incised lotus-palmette chain around the neck appear in his repertory again and again. In the name vase, Munich 1501, one even sees the conceit of the soldier on the left turning back to face the center.[62] If by him, this amphora would rank as the most outstanding example of his oeuvre.

In 1925 Mingazzini first drew attention to the iconography of Herakles Mousikos as showing the apotheosis of the hero.[63] Dugas further examined this unusual aspect of Herakles,[64] dividing the images into two groups: one which took place on Olympos and one which was terrestrial where Herakles mounts the bema in the presence of Athena and Hermes.[65] He interpreted the terrestrial scenes as an episode in the life of Herakles where this "enemy of the Muses" had to give proof of his talents on the kithara[66] in the presence of his two most sympathetic companions[67] and concluded that this new conception of Herakles must have been inspired by a poem which has not been preserved,[68] as well as by the importance of the lyre in Pythagorean philosophy.[69] Beazley, like Dugas,

pointed to a late account of Herakles as the music student of Eumolpos in the Herakliskos of Theocritus where Herakles became a bard, employing the boxwood phorminx

---

[62] I suggest that L.178 is the work of the Group of Munich 1501 and the Painter of London B 272 (separate in ABV 341–2 and combined by Beazley in Para 153–154). Villa Giulia 15534 (ABV 341, 3, Para 153, 5), Munich 1501 (ABV 341, above 1, Para 153, 4), Vatican 386 (Para 153, 11), Würzburg 202 (ABV 341, bottom Para 153, bottom), Boulogne 409 (Para 153, bottom), Bologna 22 (ABV 341, 4) are remarkably similar in several of these respects, especially in their compositional elements. Leyden PC52 (ABV 341, 2, Para 153, 3) is identical, even down to the presence of added red in the horse's mane and forelock, incisions and shape of the horse's jaw, halter, ear, bit, straight and close parallel incisions on the chest (M.B. Moore, Horses in Attic Black-Figured Vase-Painting, 1977, p.300), boxy hooves, and the detail of the Boeotian helmet and himation on the left hoplite and the lack of himation on the right hoplite. There are, however, differences, such as the shorter tear duct of the horse and single incised line for the brow, the lack of the second arc in the bi-convex arc incision high on the breast, (although these may be obscured by over-painting, ibidem, p. 305, fig.14), the presence of a straight breast band with ornaments rendered in added white and red, the different treatment of the incised reins and shoulders, added red in the tongue pattern of Leyden PC 52, the lack of a maeander frieze, and the unfinished circumscribed upright lotus bud frieze, the replacement of added red (L. 178) for added white on the helmet crests, The lack of added red in the treatment of the hoplites' greaves, the lotus-palmette chain on the neck (London B272, Munich 1574, and Leyden PC 52), the curved incision showing the horse's upper breast (Moore, op. cit., p. 301, fig. 6), the lack of the second arc in the bi-convex arc incision high on the breast (ibidem, p. 305, fig.14), the infrequency of the maeander pattern on the lower body (present on London B267 though the upright lotus bud frieze was not dotted, also not on Villa Guilia 15536 which has a bichrome tongue pattern (as do Munich 1501 and Oxford 210, ABV 341, 2 and Para 153) and seven-leafed side palmettes) and the side palmettes have seven, not five leaves (ABV 341, 1 and Para 153, 1). According to Dietrich von Bothmer, "The composition of the obverse is clearly dependent on the conceit by the Lysippides Painter in the Villa Giulia, but the execution of the drawing is on a lower level, closest to the Group of Munich 1501 and the Painter of London B 272. The neck amphora may well be by the latter artist and should rank among his more accomplished works." Letter to author March 22, 1992. See E. Künze-Gotte, Der Kleophrades Maler unten Malern: schwarzfiguren Amphoren, 1992.

[63] P. Mingazzini, La rappresentazioni vascolari del mito del'apoteosi di Herakles, Memoria della R. Accademia dei Lincei 6, 1925, p.463, nr.197–220.

[64] C. Dugas, Héraclès Mousicos, Revue des Etudes Greques 57, 1944, pp.61–70.

---

[60] Ibidem, 1–12, for the Lysippides Painter's role in establishing new and relevant Herakles iconography. For parallels in the depiction of greaves, see work by the Antimenes Painter: Vatican 392, Bürow, cit. in note 21, pl.70; Cambridge GR 32–1864, ibidem, pl.68; Rome Capitoline 88, ibidem, pl.66; Paris Matossian, ibidem, pl.33; Villa Giulia 15537, ibidem, pl.33; Würzburg L185, ibidem, pl.1; Berlin F 1842, ibidem, pl.30; Oxford 1965.116, ibidem, pl.41; London B267, ibidem, pl.40; NY 56.171.20; and the Lysippides Painter NY 58.32, 89.256 (related to the Lysippides Painter); and Cleveland 27.433, W. Moon, Ancient Greek Art and Iconography, 1983, fig. 49a; and NY 56.171.14 (in the Manner of the Lysippides Painter).

[61] See note 41.

or elaborate kithara.[70] An even later tradition mentions the fate of Herakles' ill-fated music instructor, Linus, whom Herakles killed by striking him with a lyre.[71] Probably the tradition was oral, transmitted in popular songs and lyrics by the very kitharoidoi[72] whose pose is echoed in the iconography of Herakles Kitharoidos.[73] If, in fact, the Athenian recitals did include performances of songs about Herakles, then they would have provided a vehicle for the celebration of both the city goddess and the hero of the gigantomachy. These recitals perhaps inspired this innovative portrayal of Herakles performing for the gods in the context of the festival.

Boardman has suggested that the recitals were consciously exploited by the Peisistratids, formalized in songs and hymns commissioned by the priestly families of Athens serving Peisistratos' new policies. The new iconography, where Herakles and Athena represent a significant proportion of the output of Athenian potters, reflects this activity with vase painters merely passing on new stories

through their medium.[74] In his argument for the preeminent position of Herakles in the iconography of Peisistratid Athens as well as the hero's special relationship with Athena,[75] Boardman has examined particular episodes which acquired special significance during this time, especially those which appeared for the first time or underwent change in or after the 560's.[76] One of these episodes is, in fact, Herakles Mousikos whose iconography is, moreover, exclusively Athenian, dating between 530 and the end of the sixth century B.C.[77] In these depictions the hero's patron goddess Athena is present.[78]

---

[65] Dionysos, Poseidon, and Ares also attend the spectacle (Acropolis 1207 Graef-Langlotz I p.134, pl.70.5 and London B228, Schauenburg, cit. in note 15, fig. 11). Elsewhere Hebe and Iolaos are present.

[66] Less often he plays the lyre or the pipes.

[67] Where Hebe and/or Dionysos were present, Dugas suggested an Olympian context (Dugas, cit. in note 64, p. 63, n.5). Dionysos is also present on Howard-Sneed (1985) ex Pizzati; Munich 1707, Schauenburg, cit. in note 15, p. 54, n.21, fig. 9; and Acropolis 1207 Graef-Langlotz I p.134, pl.70.5

[68] Dugas, cit. in note 64, pp. 61–70 and Beazley, cit. in note 24, p. 70.

[69] Ibidem, pp.69–70.

[70] 24.109–110. Beazley, cit. in note 23, p. 70 and Dugas, op. cit., p.65.

[71] Pseudo-Apollodorus II, 4, 9.

[72] In Boardman, cit. in note 38, pp. 68–69, M. Robertson suggests that it could refer to Homeric recitals in Athens as established by Hipparchos (Plato's Hipparchos 228B-C) and introduced for the Panathenaia.

[73] Although some performers are shown mounting the bema as on L.176 and the kithara player on Harvard 1977.21.62397 (Shapiro, cit. in note 6, fig. 49a), most are depicted as already standing on it (Lysippides Painter: Louvre G1 (ibidem, fig. 44); Walters 48.2107 (ibidem, fig. 46); NY 07.286.72 (G. Pinney and B. Ridgway Aspects of Ancient Art, 1979, pp.60–61, cat. no. 27); as well as the later red-figured vase by the Peleus Painter: Agora P 27349 (Holloway, cit. in note 12).

[74] Boardman, cit. in note 47, p. 247 and Boardman, Herakles, Peisistratos, and the Unconvinced, Journal of Hellenic Studies 109, 1989, p.158.

Since the tendency in the fifth century was to assimilate material concerning Herakles to Theseus, it is interesting that we have no extant Theseus Mousikos. Boardman suggests that the reason is that Herakles was a mortal hero with whom mortals could identify (cit. in note 47, p. 247). Or was it rather the strong Peisistratid connection with the kitharodic competitions at the Panathenaia that made this association less desirable? I have already mentioned the decline in frequency of images of competing kitharists and kitharodes after 500 B.C.

[75] Ibidem. Regarding Herakles' promotion to divine status, Diodorus (4, 39) states that the Athenians first persuaded the rest of the world of Herakles' divinity. Moreover, Pausanias (1, 15, 3) asserts that he was first worshipped as a god at Marathon. Herakles and the Bull: ABV 385, 29 and 385, 30. Herakles and the Kerynitian Hind: Toledo 1958.69, Para 168, 2bis, Herakles wrestling down the Nemean Lion: Vatican 417, ABV 384, 26; Altenburg 221, ABV 383, 7; Herakles petting Kerberos: Amiens ABV 384, 25; and Louvre F 241, ABV 383, 5 as well as more traditional scenes of Herakles and Apollo fighting over the tripod, etc. This last image could in fact be seen as a struggle for preeminence of Peisistratid Athens (Herakles) vs. Delphi (Apollo).

[76] He elucidates equivalences between Peisistratos and Herakles in the Phye episode (Herodotos 1, 60) and the rash of scenes with the apotheosis of Herakles in the second half of the sixth century B.C. He stresses the role of Herakles in defeating the giants in the gigantomachy which helped Zeus/Athena come to power and shows a scene from this subject where Herakles accompanies Athena in her chariot (Vatican 381 ABV 671) Furthermore, Herakles asserts his prominent place in gigantomachies from the third quarter of the sixth century (Boardman, cit. in note 38, pp. 62–69). Elsewhere he states that "The hero had...signified Athena and Athens as much as Peisistratos and his family." Herakles, Theseus, and the Amazons, in The Eye of Greece: Studies in the Art of Athens D. Kurtz and B. Sparkes, eds., 1982, p.4.

[77] Boardman, cit. in note 37, pp. 10–11, cit. in note 47, pp. 245–46, and Schauenburg, cit. in note 15.

Schauenburg has studied vases depicting Herakles Mousikos, one of which is the pointed amphora of Panathenaic shape by the Acheloos Painter with Herakles Auletes performing for two gentlemen wearing wreaths of knotted sticks as do the witnesses on L. 176.[79] Schauenburg has divided the extant scenes into five categories, the fifth of which is Herakles playing while mounting the bema, as on L. 178.[80] This last group relies heavily on the iconography of the Panathenaic Festival (as evidenced by L. 176): in the presence of the bema, the stance and gesture of Herakles, and the witnesses – divine audience members or judges, seated or standing.[81] L. 178 belongs to this critical group with Herakles mounting the competition platform, arguing a Panathenaic context.[82]

Schauenburg supports Boardman's association of the appearance of this motif in black figure with the institution of the mousikoi agones of the Panathenaic Festival under the sons of Peisistratos, particularly with Hipparchos' introduction of Homeric recitals into the Panathenaia.[83] He asserts that the concert of the hero was transferred from earth (Athens) to Olympos. The event could be taking place in Peisistratid Athens in the context of the Panathenaia with the other gods in attendance such as in the later Parthenon frieze.[84] In this way, the hero serves Peisistratid Kulturpolitik,[85] flattering the tyrants, by rendering the Panathenaia so important under Peisis-

---

[78] There are two occurrences where Herakles mounts the bema alone (Paris, Louvre Cp1107 and Oxford 211, ABV 484, 9), but this does not make sense in the context of a contest or performance. On Oxford 211 by the Edinburgh Painter Herakles mounts the bema alone ABV 484, 9. The bema has the same shape as that at Dunedin and Tarquinia 681, except it has two incised divisions. B: satyr reclines on altar, piping flutes. 2) On neck amphora Louvre Cp 10017 Herakles is shown mounting the bema alone (Para 219, 133 (Schauenburg, cit. in note 15, fig. 6).

[79] London BM 167, ABV 382, 1. But on it there is no bema. On the reverse Herakles appears with a bull, while Hermes plays on a lyre with a goat.

[80] Schauenburg, cit. in note 15, pp. 49–76. Of his 38 black-figured representations, at least 11 fall into the 5th group. See below. Hermes, frequently shown, is omitted on L.178 and replaced by the less common but logical Dionysos. This is no surprise, as he would be a natural to preside over performances of a dramatic nature. The Dionysiac figures of Orpheus and silens also occasionally mount the bema to perform, in images strikingly similar to contemporary scenes of kitharodes of the Panathenaia (ibidem, p. 65 and Shapiro, cit. in note 6, p. 69). Their significance is unclear.

[81] These features can be seen on numerous black-figured vases, of which twelve show him mounting the bema with an audience present, two show him mounting the bema without an audience, and one shows him already standing on the bema with an audience. 1) Herakles mounts the bema while Athena sits on a lekythos, Vienna 75, ABV 379, 270. 2) On neck amphora Vienna IV 1001, Herakles is shown mounting while Athena stands by. The bema has two divisions (Schauenburg, cit. in note 15, fig. 13). 3) On the Acheloos Painter's neck amphora, Howard-Sneed (1985) ex Pizzati, ABV 370, 134, the bema has three horizontal incised divisions. Herakles is shown mounting and Athena and Dionysos stand while Hebe(?) sits. On reverse: Dionysos, two satyrs and a female. 4) On the Acheloos Painter's pointed amphora of Panathenaic shape Munich SL 459, ABV 369, 121, Herakles mounts a bema with three incised divisions. Hermes and Athena are standing. Dionysos and satyrs are on the reverse. 5) On Louvre neck amphora fragments Herakles is shown mounting the bema with Athena and Hermes present. B: Dionysos and maenads, ABV 370, 133. 6) On Dunedin E 48.226, ABV 386, 12, dependent on the Antimenes Painter, Herakles is shown mounting between a standing Athena and Hermes. The bema is squat with a shallow protruding cap. B: warrior with old man and woman. 7) On neck amphora in the Manner of the Antimenes Painter Boulogne 78 ABV 277, 17, Herakles is shown mounting while Athena and Hermes stand. A wide, two-stepped bema is shown (Schauenburg, op. cit., fig. 14). B: fight between two mounted warriors over a fallen warrior. 8) On the neck amphora Munich 1575, ABV 256, 16, by the Lysippides Painter Herakles is shown mounting in the presence of Athena. The bema is boxy with no incised divisions. B: two warriors in frontal quadriga. 9) On the neck amphora in the private Swiss collection Herakles and Athena are both shown mounting a boxy bema with one incised division. B: Hermes with a lyre, Dionysos, silen (Schauenburg, op. cit., figs.1–4). 10) On the neck amphora Tarquinia 681 Herakles is shown mounting and Athena standing. The bema has three steps. B: Hermes and Poseidon. 11) On the neck amphora in a Swiss private collection Herakles is shown mounting between Athena and Hermes who are standing. B: warrior departing. Para 184, 9bis (Schauenburg, op. cit., figs. 15, 16). 12) On the belly amphora by the Lysippides Painter at the Villa Giulia (24998) Herakles is shown mounting with Athena and Hermes seated. The boxy bema has three divisions. B: warrior with horse, old man and woman. (Beazley, cit. in note 23, pl. 79: 3,4).

On a neck amphora Worcester 1966.63 Herakles is shown already standing on the bema flanked by Hermes and Athena who sit. The bema has three steps. B: Herakles fights Kyknos while Athena and Ares stand nearby (D. Buitron, *Attic Vases in New England Collections*, 1972, pp. 48–49). Although not necessarily related to the scenes with bema present, on Tarquinia 679 Herakles stands next to a burning altar surrounded by a seated Hebe, and standing Iolaos and Athena. The altar has the same shape as the bema from Oxford and Dunedin E 48.226.

tratos and his sons, that it in turn elevated Athens itself to the stature of Olympos.

The amusical hero is equally elevated by his patrons to contend with divine musicians. On a neck amphora in a Swiss private collection Athena participates, simultaneously mounting the bema opposite Herakles for a duet.[86] If the scene of Herakles Kitharoidos is to be interpreted simply as a concert, then Herakles is playing for the gods in the context of the Panathenaia. Yet if, in the case of Schauenburg's type five (with the bema), it can be further interpreted as a contest, then one must ask with whom does Herakles compete? Boardman has inferred that he competes with Apollo, for by using Apollo's instrument Herakles is usurping his role,[87] interesting, considering the competitive context of the Panathenaic Festival. To my knowledge Apollo never attends Herakles' performances, nor do black-figured vases depict Apollo Kitharoidos performing on the bema.[88] This may reflect a certain tension between Athens (Herakles) and Delphi (Apollo) in the sixth century. The earlier iconography of Herakles and Apollo struggling for the tripod is well-known, and Boardman has elucidated its significance. Here, perhaps just as Herakles stole Apollo's tripod in the other agon, he is attempting to master or even steal his sacred instrument as well.[89] It has been suggested that the goal of this Peisistratid patronage was to elevate the Pana-

thenaic games to the level of the Pythian musical competitions in honor of Apollo at Delphi.[90] Here one may see this competition for glory played out in the medium of vase-painting.

These two vases can now be added to the corpus of mortal and divine performance scenes associated with the institution of the mousikoi agones of the Panathenaic Festival under Peisistratos and his sons. They give additional evidence concerning the borrowing of iconography from mortal performances for the depiction of the gods and heroes. Furthermore, they can be used to infer tension between Peisistratid Athens and Delphi in the sixth century through the vying of Herakles and Apollo. They depict the trickle-down effect of the tyrants' agenda on the vase painters' world depicting a Panathenaia in the legendary past where all of the gods or a select few would have been present to bear witness to the glories of Athens, commemorated and perhaps exploited in historic times by the tyrant Peisistratos and his sons. In this way the iconography of Herakles Kitharoidos (ca. 530–500 B.C.), based on that of mortal competitors, simultaneously flattered and symbolized the tyrant and his/their aggrandizement of their city through the musical competitions of the Panathenaia.

---

[82] Boardman, cit. in note 37, pp. 10–11. Schauenburg cites as many as seventy examples of musicians on the bema (cit. in note 15, p. 67). Of the approximately 35 black figure representations, more than half show the kithara player. The rest depict auletes. They are more long-lived and more plentiful than those showing Herakles Mousikos, and thus the iconography must be derived from them and not vice-versa (ibidem, p. 66).

[83] Boardman, op. cit, pp. 10–11. "…the scheme of Herakles on the bema is derived from images of mortal competitions, which, when possible to localize, are to be connected with the Panathenaia" (Schauenburg op. cit., p. 73). See note 36.

[84] Perikles and Phidias were certainly not the first to glorify Athens and Athenians.

[85] Boardman, cit. in note 74, p. 159.

[86] Schauenburg, cit. in note 15, figs. 1, 2.

[87] Boardman, cit. in note 47, p. 246.

[88] Although he does appear on a red-figured example in Boston (ARV² 1107.6, Schauenburg, cit. in note 15, p.73).

[89] Maas and Snyder, cit. in note 8, p.57.

[90] See Donald Kyle on competition in prize-giving between the games, Gifts and Glory: Panathenaic Prize Amphoras and the History of Greek Athletic Prizes in Neils, cit. in note 6. For the special prominence of music at Delphi, see Shapiro in Neils, op. cit., p.57, n.30 and J. Herington, Poetry into Drama, 1985, pp.161–165.

Fig. 2. Side B of L. 176. Kitharode in performance.

**Fig. 1.** Black-figure amphora by the Acheloos Painter. Side A. Kitharode in performance. From a private collection – currently on view at The Breakers, Newport, Rhode Island, L. 176. Courtesy of the Preservation Society of Newport County.

**Fig. 3.** Black-figure amphora belonging to the Group of Munich 1501. Side A. Herakles Kitharoidos with Hermes and Athena. From a private collection – currently on view at The Breakers, Newport, Rhode Island, L.178. Courtesy of the Preservation Soceity of Newport County.

**Fig. 4.** Side B of L. 178. Mounted horseman, warriors, and hounds.

# ARCHAIC BILLBOARDS:
# THE HERMS OF HIPPARCHOS AND
# THE PROPAGANDA OF WISDOM
# IN ARCHAIC GREECE

*Derek B. Counts*

An earlier version of this paper was presented at the annual meeting of the Archaeological Institute of America (San Diego, 1995). I am honored to be part of this volume and would like to thank Professor Holloway for his role in the development of this article and for his contagious enthusiasm for Archaic Greece. I would also like to thank Alan Boegehold and Michael Toumazou for their helpful suggestions. I owe a special note of gratitude to Brian Lavelle for his insightful criticisms and support throughout the evolution of this article.

According to the Hipparchos, a Pseudo-Platonic dialogue dating to the fourth century BC, Hipparchos, son of the Athenian tyrant Peisistratos,

> set up figures of Hermes along the roads in the midst of the city and every district town; and then, after selecting from his own wise lore, both learnt from others and discovered for himself, the things that he considered the wisest, he threw these into elegiac form and inscribed them on the figures as verses of his own and testimonies of his wisdom…There are two such inscriptions of his: on the left side of each Hermes there is one in which the god says that he stands in the midst of the city and the township, while on the right side he says:
>
> > The memorial of Hipparchus: walk with
> > just intent.
>
> There are many other fine inscriptions from his poems on other figures of Hermes, and this one, in particular, on the Steiria road, in which he says:
>
> > The memorial of Hipparchus: deceive not
> > a friend (Hipp, 228c–229b).[1]

That such a program existed is supported by later ancient sources,[2] as well as an example of such a herm found in Koropi. In 1937, Kirchner and Dow published an inscription from this fragmentary herm, dating to the late sixth century BC:

> Bright Hermes in between Kephale and the
> city.[3]

In a rare consensus of text and artifact, the fragment's inscription authenticates the account of Hipparchos' herms in the passage above; moreover, traces of anathyrosis on the top of the shaft suggest the presence of an attached head strengthening the case for a herm.[4] In an essay probing the extent of political propaganda in the sixth century BC, Martin Nilsson pondered the medium for propaganda in this period, noting that, "In antiquity a

---

[1] Translation from W. R. M. Lamb, Plato Vol. XII, 1927.

[2] E.g., Harpokration and Photios; see R. E. Wycherley, The Athenian Agora III: Literary and Epigraphical Testimonia, 1957, nos. 305 and 308.

[3] J. Kirchner and S. Dow, Inschriften vom Attischen Lande, AM, 62, 1937, p. 1–3. Also published in CAH2 IV, 293 (fig. 29); IG I3 1023; CEG I.304.

[4] S. Miller, The Altar of the Six Goddesses in Thessalian Pherai, ClAnt, 7, 1974, p. 248–9. For general treatments of Greek herms, as well as those attributed to Hipparchos, see R. Lullies, Die Typen der Griechischen Herme, 1931; J. Crome, Hipparcheioi Hermai, AM, 60–61, 1935–1936, p. 300–13; H. Goldman, The Origin of the Greek Herm, AJA, 46, 1942, p. 58–68; E. B. Harrison, The Athenian Agora XI: Archaic and Archaistic Sculpture, Princeton, 1965, p. 108–42; H. Wrede, Die Antike Herm, Mainz, 1985; B. Lavelle, Hipparchos' Herms, EMC, 29, 1985, p. 411–20; A. Ford, The Seal of Theognis: The Politics of Authorship in Archaic Greece, in T. F. Figueira and G. Nagy, eds., Theognis of Megara: Poetry and the Polis, Baltimore, 1986, p. 82–95; R. Osborne, The Erection and Mutilation of the Hermai, PCPS, 31, 1986, p. 47–73; and H. A. Shapiro, Art and Cult Under the Tyrants in Athens, Mainz, 1989, p. 125–32.

means of communication was lacking which is all important nowadays, the printed word. There were no newspapers, no printed pamphlets, and no posters."[5] Hipparchos' herms and their inscribed maxims answered this problem and represent a striking example in Archaic Greece where literary propaganda merges with a sculpted image, for a seemingly political purpose and in a seemingly explicit manner.

The seventh and sixth centuries BC are characterized by a flurry of apothegmatic maxims and anecdotes attributed to political leaders that defined wisdom and communicated power. Political power and intellectual power were viewed as codependent.[6] In particular, tyrants and other civic leaders were immortalized through a tradition of sagacious maxims attributed to them by ancient authors. It is within this socio-political construct that Hipparchos' elegiac maxims and his motives for propagating his own wisdom should be placed. Rather than reserving his favorite bits of wisdom for a limited audience, Hipparchos chose to publicize his message on roadside herms – a message signed by Hipparchos' own name and conveyed through the god Hermes. This paper will consider the nature of poetic maxims and their link to conceptions of wisdom in Archaic Greece and, more specifically, Hipparchos' unique appropriation of this literary (and oracular) tradition for his herms.

B. Lavelle has suggested that Hipparchos' maxims "soothed [the countryfolk] by the omnipresence of moral philosophy in Solon's mode".[7] The prominent role of poetry in Solon's regime certainly influenced Hipparchos' choice of poetic verse as the medium for propagating his wisdom. The Peisistratid court, however, was no less interested in the literary arts; Simonides of Keos and Anakreon of Teos were brought to Athens by the tyrants and Hipparchos' own role in the standardization of Homeric poetry is well attested.[8] In general, Greek lyric poetry offered an effective medium for political expression and archaic poets freely tested the effectiveness of poetry as a means of propaganda. Alkaios' opposition to the tyrant Pittakos and his use of verse as a medium for challenging the tyrant is clear from several fragments that issued forceful and moralizing invective.

> …But Potbelly Pittakos did not speak to their
> souls but casually
> tramples oaths underfoot and now he devours
> our city…(129)[9]
>
> They made that bastard Pittakos tyrant of this
> lily-livered luckless city
> and now in throngs they praise him to the
> skies (348).

Theognis addressed a similar situation in Megara where the political upheavals following the tyranny of Theagenes and the emergence of the nouveau riche threatened the power of the old aristocratic families.

> Kyrnos, this city's with child. I fear that she'll
> bring forth a chastiser of our evil violence,
> for though the citizens are sensible, their leaders are on their way to enormous wickedness.
> Kyrnos, never yet have its nobles destroyed a
> city, but whenever violence pleases the
> base, and they
> corrupt the commons and give judgment to
> unjust men for the sake of power and private gain, do not
> expect that city to be untroubled for long, not
> even if now she lies under tranquility,
> whenever these to evil men become dear-
> gains that come to the common folk for
> ill.
> From such come revolutions and internecine
> gore and tyrannies. Our city may these
> never please (39–52).

It is clear that poets such as Solon, Alkaios and Theognis employed their verse as a forum for political didacticism and moralizing. Archaic lyric poetry is saturated with a variety of themes, yet the commingling of poetry and politics was conspicuous and constant.

[5] M. P. Nilsson, Political Propaganda in Sixth Century Athens, in G. Mylonas, ed. Studies Presented to David Moore Robinson on his Seventieth Birthday, Saint Louis, 1951–1953, p. 743.

[6] Cf., Plut. Them. 2 where the author defines Themistokles' 'wisdom' as a combination of political skill and practical intelligence. Plutarch credits the creation of this distinct combination to Solon.

[7] Lavelle, cit. in note 4, p. 419.

[8] Arist. Ath. Pol. 18.1 and [Plato] Hipp. 229a–b. For a recent appraisal of Hipparchos' role in the patronage of poets and literature, see H. A. Shapiro, Hipparchos and the Rhapsodes, in C. Dougherty and L. Kurke, eds., Cultural Poetics in Archaic Greece, Oxford, 1993, p. 92–107.

[9] All translations and fragment references of the archaic poets are from B. Fowler, Archaic Greek Poetry, 1992.

While the role of archaic lyric poetry in the party politics of the Archaic period should not be disregarded, Hipparchos condensed and simplified his message in the form of slogan-like, elegiac maxims. Focusing on the significance of 'wisdom speech' in Greek prose, Russo has argued that rural peoples, or 'rustics', were especially attracted to maxims and would often use them in their everyday speech.[10] As brief testimonies of universal truths, proverbs and maxims become an ideal embodiment of a sort of 'cosmetic' wisdom that can be understood and exploited by a wide range of people. In light of this, Hipparchos' choice of the maxim may have been deemed especially suitable for demonstrating his wisdom to the audience traveling to and from the city. In fact, brief mottoes and slogans were marked characteristics of the so-called "Epoch of the Seven Sages" and the subsequent contest of wisdom in the seventh and sixth centuries. The controversy surrounding the chronology and composition of the actual Sages has been incessant.[11] In the context discussed here however, we must only believe that the 'concept' of the sage was omnipresent in Archaic Greek society (i.e., a public perception that wisdom equals power personified in certain leaders); the need for an established, recognized, or even codified college of seven seems irrelevant. The mere fact that ancient authors were confused as to who was and was not included among the seven betrays a more universal conception of the link between wisdom and the personae of key figures during the Archaic period. Whether the Seven Sages actually produced and preached wise maxims or, more likely, the examples of their wisdom reflect an archaizing, mytho-historical construction, the association of intellectual skill with political leaders seems

well established by the last quarter of the sixth century BC.

The profusion of maxims among the accounts of political 'sages' suggests a symbiotic relationship between the claim to wisdom and the claim to power in the seventh and sixth centuries. Tyrants and other leading men of the Archaic period, some of whom were later included among the Seven Sages, were commonly attributed maxims that became symbols of their wisdom. In an effort to address traditional notions of wisdom in Archaic Greece, Martin has isolated three 'features' common to the so-called sages: poetry, politics, and performance.[12] The biographical accounts of men such as Thales, Solon, Kleoboulos, and Pittakos possess elements of each feature and constitute a model for characterizing wisdom during the Archaic period. One can readily distinguish the same elements in Hipparchos and his herms: a) Hipparchos was eminently political as tyrant of Athens, b) his maxims, despite their mundane nature, are poetry, and c) with Hermes as proxy, Hipparchos 'performed' for every traveler as he engaged them with a blend of practical information and advice. Viewed within this model, Hipparchos' herms self-consciously embrace the concept of wisdom as an archaic institution and symbol of practical skill.[13]

Hipparchos' simplification of archaic poetics into motto-like quips of wisdom complemented his attempts to associate himself with the wisest and most powerful men of Greece. Peisistratos himself had laid the foundations for the family's claim to wisdom a few years prior by deceiving the Athenians in several episodes.[14] McGlew has noted that stories such as these "clung to tyrants" and that "the common perception of their extraordinary acuity" explains why certain men were touted as "models of political and practical wisdom".[15] Not trusting the endurance of popular opinion, Hipparchos apparently hoped to affirm his own claim to wisdom and build upon the foundations laid by his father.

---

[10] J. Russo, Prose Genres for the Performance of Traditional Wisdom in Ancient Greece: Proverb, Maxim, Apothegm, in L. Edmonds and R. Wallace, eds., Poet, Public and Performance in Ancient Greece, 1997, p. 55–7.

[11] For the Sages as a specific group, see W. Wiersma, The Seven Sages and the Prize of Wisdom, Mnemosyne, Ser. 3.1–2, 1933–1935, p. 150–4; B. Snell, Zur Geschichte vom Gastmal der sieben Weisen, in O. Hiltbrunner, ed., Thesaurismata, Munich, 1954, p. 105–11; O. Barkowski, Sieben Weise, RE, 2nd ser., 1972, col. 2242–64; A. Mosshammer, The Epoch of the Seven Sages, ClAnt, 9, 1976, p. 165–80; D. Fehling, Die Sieben Weisen und die fruhgriechische Chronologie: Eine traditions-geschichtliche Studie, Bern, 1985; R. P. Martin, The Seven Sages as Performers of Wisdom, in C. Dougherty and L. Kurke, eds., Cultural Poetics in Archaic Greece, Oxford, 1993, p. 108–28.

[12] Martin, cit. in note 11, p. 113.

[13] Ibidem, p. 123–4.

[14] Herodotus recounts the story of Peisistratos' 'divinely-sanctioned' return to Athens in the company of a tall countrywoman dressed in the guise of Athena (I.60). Another story reveals how Peisistratos disarmed a throng of Athenians by a 'clever' trick (Arist. Ath. Pol. 15.4).

[15] J. F. McGlew, Tyranny and Political Culture in Ancient Greece, 1993, p. 29.

Despite the commonplace character of their 'wise' maxims and 'intellectual' exploits, political moguls such as Periander of Corinth, Pittakos of Mytilene, Bias of Priene and Solon of Athens were revered as the wisest of all men and remained so among ancient authors. In light of this intimate relationship between power and perceived wisdom, it is not surprising that a plethora of wise sayings and moralizing slogans attributed to these political sages have been handed down by ancient sources. Archaic poets such as Alkaios and Simonides preserve bits of wisdom attributed to the political 'sages' and, consequently, reinforce the presence of political and moral wisdom among accounts of archaic statesmen.[16] Alkaios writes

> Once, Aristodemos, they say,
> at Sparta said a very clever thing:
> "Money's the man." No one poor
> is either noble or in honor held.

Similarly, Simonides writes

> …nor does Pittakos' maxim harmonize
> with mine, although spoken by a wise man.
> He said, "Hard to be good."
> God alone could have this prize…(542).

Diogenes Laertius, in his biographies of the Seven Sages, not only recounts anecdotes of their civil achievements, but also provides maxims which read like 'calling-cards' for each of the various wise men (e.g., To Periander is attributed, "Practice makes perfect" and Bias said, "Most men are bad") reflecting the continuation of a literary tradition of associating archaic political sages with short, slogan-like aphorisms disguised as wisdom.[17]

The role of prominent, civic leaders within this genre of archaic slogans cannot be overlooked; the impetus for

these 'sign-posts of wisdom' is derived not only from the contest of wisdom, but also the quest for power and political ascendancy in the Archaic period. The examples above illustrate an ancient connection between the leader and motto, between politics and wisdom – a connection that Hipparchos appears to have realized and exploited. This becomes apparent when we consider that Hipparchos signed each maxim to insure that his name be connected to these tokens of wisdom. Similar to the poet's sphragis, Hipparchos offered a visible 'seal' of ownership of this wisdom. In a discussion of the politics of poetic sophia (or skill) in Archaic Greece, Ford compares the sphragis of Theognis to the maxims of Hipparchos, noting that this seal did not always signify authorship of the poetry, but rather emphasizes the attachment of the verse to a particular name.[18] Thus, Hipparchos' sphragis need not denote original authorship; rather, it empowers Hipparchos as the 'owner' of a particular text and, therefore, beneficiary of any of its perceived intellectual, moral or political power. As Ford notes, "the essence of Hipparchus' and Theognis' sophia is the same: a mastery of poetic discourse enabling one to express the esteemed behavior of the community".[19] By instituting a corpus of his own mottoes, Hipparchos laid claim to his legitimacy as a 'sage' in the sixth century and, in effect, supplied a visible manifestation of his sapience.

The use of wisdom as a political tool was commonplace to tyrants and other leading figures of the Archaic period. Hipparchos' attempts to associate himself with this style of political 'sloganizing', and his choice of the herm as the medium clearly support his hopes of glorifying the Peisistratid tyranny in Athens and legitimizing their control over all of Attica. As opposed to the songs and sayings of other archaic politicians and poets, Hipparchos was able to publicize his own mottoes through the written word (i.e. not relying upon word of mouth) to all of Attica. More importantly, Hipparchos chose to monumentalize this wisdom, permanently, by inscribing his maxims on herms. When contextualized within the archaic conventions of wisdom and its affinity to political ascendancy, Hipparchos' program of road-side herms finds a happy niche where mottoes were kept in front of the lêos by political leaders of the Archaic period.

---

[16] Although not attached to particular persons, similar examples of this brand of 'wisdom' are preserved in various fragments from archaic poets. E.g., Alkman, "Of Persuasion and Order the sister, Of Forethought the daughter" (64) and Praxilla, "Beware, my friend, beneath every stone a scorpion" (750).

[17] For Thales, cf. I.22–44; Solon, cf. I.45–67; Chilon, cf. I.68–73; Pittakos, cf. I.74–81; Bias, cf. I.82–88; Kleoboulos, cf. I.89–93; Periander, cf. I.94–100.That this relationship was preserved well beyond the Archaic period is shown by a collection of herms found in the so-called Villa of Brutus in Tivoli which are now in the Vatican. Discovered in 1774, these herms represent one of the chief ensembles of the Seven Sages that have survived from the ancient world. See G. M. A. Richter, Portraits of the Greeks, 1965, p. 81–91.

[18] Ford, cit. in note 4, p. 88.

[19] Ibidem.

# FEMALE SEXUALITY AND DANAE AND THE GOLDEN RAIN

*Frances Van Keuren*

This paper was originally delivered at the colloquium "Image and Medium in Ancient Art and Coinage" honoring R. Ross Holloway at the annual meeting of the Archaeological Institute of America, New York, December 29th, 1996. The undergraduate and graduate students who took my mythology course in spring 1999 – ARHI 4030/6030, The Classical Tradition in the Visual Arts – at the University of Georgia gave me many good ideas about the calyx crater (Fig. 1) during class discussion. Prof. R. Ross Holloway, Brown University; Prof. Brian E. McConnell, Emory University; Prof. Jenifer Neils, Case Western Reserve University; Prof. John H. Oakley, College of William and Mary; and Dr. Emma J. Stafford, University of Wales, Lampeter, kindly read the manuscript and offered invaluable suggestions in regard to additional bibliography and ways to recast and reshape parts of it. Mary Jones, hairdresser at Hair Designers in Athens, Georgia, generously made time to go over my discussion of Fig. 1 and demonstrate what she felt Danae and the bride were doing with their fillets in Figs. 1 and 2 (see Figs. 3–4).

---

Most ancient authors report that Zeus became the father of Perseus the Gorgon-slayer by bursting into Danae's chamber of imprisonment in the form of golden rain.[1] Modern scholars have variously interpreted this fantastic story. For example, Mary Bly offered the following observations:[2]

> Of the forms Jupiter adopts, the rain of gold is the most directly sexual: in its downward movement, its liquid properties, its fertility (evidenced by the birth of Perseus), and its suggestive arrival in Danae's lap. The rain of gold presents itself as instantaneous consummation, the body metamorphosed into a sexual weapon…In a sense, the Danae myth is a perfect metaphor for rape (violation without consent or affection), and it sits uneasily in an amorous context.[3]

In The Reign of the Phallus: Sexual Politics in Ancient Athens, Eva C. Keuls described Zeus as "the master rapist", and observed: "In the literary tradition, Zeus overcomes most of his female victims by trickery: he rapes Leda in the form of a swan, Danaë in the guise of a golden rain, and Alkmene in the persona of her legitimate husband."[4] Later on in the same well-known study, Keuls characterized Danae as "the victim of rape by Zeus."[5] Walter Burkert included the Danae tale in a "set of apparently unrelated myths [that] can be analyzed as covering the same basic structure…the tales told adapt themselves neatly to a sequence of five 'functions,' easy to understand, which I would call 'the girl's tragedy'."[6] According to this schema, function number five consists of the following: "Rape: the girl is surprised, violated, and impregnated by a god – it is Zeus for Callisto, Danaë, Io, and Antiope, Poseidon for Tyro and Melanippe, Heracles for Auge."[7]

Other scholars have been more cautious in characterizing the amorous encounters of the gods with mortals as rape. Mary Lefkowitz challenges "the common assumption that Greek mythology effectively validates the practice of rape and approves of the violent mistreatment of women…the gods see to it that the experience, however transient, is pleasant for mortals."[8] Ellen Reeder observed that "ancient sources leave little doubt that Danae was responsive to Zeus' overture."[9] Adele Scafuro investigated

---

[1] For a summary of the literary sources on the Danae myth, which includes a discussion of the variant (attributed to Pindar and others, and repeated by Apollodoros) that the princess was seduced by her uncle Proitos, see T. Gantz, Early Greek Myth: A Guide to Literary and Artistic Sources, 1993, p. 299–303.

[2] Mary Bly, Bait for the Imagination: Danae and Consummation in Petrarch and Heywood, Comparative Literature Studies 32, 1995, p. 343–359.

[3] Ibidem, p. 343.

[4] Eva C. Keuls, The Reign of the Phallus: Sexual Politics in Ancient Athens, 2nd ed. 1993, p. 51.

[5] Ibidem, p. 340.

[6] Walter Burkert, Structure and History in Greek Mythology and Ritual, 1979, p. 6–7.

[7] Ibidem, p. 7.

[8] Seduction and Rape in Greek Myth, in Consent and Coercion to Sex and Marriage in Ancient and Medieval Societies, A.E. Laiou, ed., 1993, p. 17.

"a number of Greek myths about virgins who have pre-marital sexual relations with gods [and who] share a basic pattern which Walter Burkert has called 'the girl's trage-dy'."[10] While most of her article tried to establish different heroines' negative responses to their rapes by gods or heroes, she admitted that "there was not an inflexible paradigm that required the girls of our myths to resist the gods." As an example of non-resistance to divine amorous interest, she cited the story of Tyro and Poseidon.[11] Among her translations of literary passages, she included several describing Zeus' sexual union with Danae, but did not discuss them in the article.[12]

One of the Danae passages that Scafuro translates is this quotation from the 5th-century Athenian historian Pherekydes: "And she welcomed (ὑποδέχεται) into her lap [sc. Zeus likened unto gold], and Zeus, having revealed himself, united (μίγνυται) with the girl."[13] This passage seems to indicate that like Tyro, Danae did not resist Zeus' amorous attentions. The Pherekydes quotation, from a commentary on Apollonios Rhodios' Argonautica, also describes the events leading up to Zeus' inventive method of entering Danae's chamber. The author recounts how Danae's father Akrisios received a prophecy from the Delphic oracle that not only would he fail to have a son himself, as desired, but also his daughter would have one who would kill him. Pherekydes' account continues:

> So he went home to Argos and built a bronze chamber underground in the courtyard of his house (θάλαμον ποιεῖ χαλκοῦν ἐν τῆι αὐλῆι τῆς οἰκίας κατὰ γῆς), and there he put Danae and her nurse and kept her there so that she might not bear a son. But Zeus fell in love with

the maiden and descended from the roof in a shower of gold.[14]

Pherekydes is not the only ancient author to use the word thalamos to describe Danae's underground chamber. Significantly, the Chorus in Sophocles' Antigone refers to Danae's chamber with the same noun. In this famous ode that immediately follows Antigone's final speech, the Chorus compares Antigone's fate with that of Danae, referring to the latter's chamber of confinement as τυμβήρης θάλαμος.[15] In a convincing analysis of the Chorus' use of mythological comparisons as a means to comprehend Antigone's fate, A.S. Mc Devitt observes:

> Antigone had made much of the fact that she must die unmarried…The only marriage Antigone will know is with Hades, her only bridal-song a dirge. Thus the phrase τυμβήρης θάλαμος ("tomb-like bridal-chamber"), used to describe Danae's prison, was surely suggested by subconscious pressure from both directions; that is, by Antigone's prior emphasis on the equation of tomb and bridal-chamber, as well as by the literal appropriateness of the phrase to Danae, anticipating her impregnation by Zeus.[16]

Writing two centuries after Sophocles, Asklepiades describes Danae's quarters as χάλκειοι θάλαμοι,[17] and Pausanias calls her chamber ὁ χαλκοῦς θάλαμος.[18] If Mc Devitt has correctly understood Danae's thalamos in the Antigone as a bridal chamber, then the possibility should be explored that the word has the same significance in Pherekydes, Asklepiades and Pausanias.

The word has previously been interpreted in the other sense that θάλαμος commonly conveys, i.e. a room within the women's apartment. In their commentary on As-

---

[9] Ellen D. Reeder et alii, Pandora: Women in Classical Greece, 1995, p. 267.

[10] Adele Scafuro, Discourses of Sexual Violation in Mythic Accounts and Dramatic Versions of "The Girl's Tragedy," Differences: A Journal of Feminist Cultural Studies 2, 1990, p. 126.

[11] Ibidem, p. 133. To be added to the cited literary sources that recount Tyro's felicitous encounter with Poseidon is the famous passage in Homer, Odyssey 11.248–250, which Lefkowitz, "Seduction and Rape in Greek Myth," cit. in note 8, p. 22–23, quotes and discusses.

[12] Ibidem, p. 129–130.

[13] Scafuro, op. cit., p. 129.

[14] The English translation of the Pherekydes quotation is from J.M. Woodward, Perseus: A Study in Greek Art and Legend, 1937, p. 5. The passage in the original Greek is from Schol. Apoll. Rhod. IV 1091, in F. Jacoby, Die Fragmente der griechischen Historiker, pt. 1: Genealogie und Mythographie, A Text, 1957, no. 3, frg. 10, p. 61.

[15] Sophocles, Antigone 946.

[16] A.S. Mc Devitt, Mythological Exempla in the Fourth Stasimon of Sophocles' Antigone, Wiener Studien 103, 1990, p. 36.

[17] A.S.F. Gow and D.L. Page, eds., The Greek Anthology: Hellenistic Epigrams, vol. 1, 1965, p. 47, no. XI; and vol. 2, 1965, p. 124, commentary.

[18] Pausanias 2.23.7.

klepiades' epigram, Gow and Page insisted that Danae's chamber "is called θάλαμος elsewhere…in the sense of *inner* or *women's room* rather than *bridal chamber*," but then went on to admit that "διὰ θαλάμων ἔδυς [the words addressed by Asklepiades to Zeus] in the sense merely of *penetrated the chamber* is hard to parallel."[19] However, if bridal chamber was the intended significance for thalamos in all the cited passages, then the difficulty of conceiving of Zeus as penetrating the chamber is eliminated; for then thalamos can be understood as a metaphor for Danae's penetrated body. And her sexual experience within the chamber would be likened to that of the bride when she and her groom consummated their marriage. Since a bride consented to becoming a sexual partner of her groom, Danae's consent to Zeus' visitation would be implied. Understanding thalamos as a bridal chamber appears to rule out the possibility that Danae was raped.

Bridal references and other pictorial devices that imply Danae's consent to impregnation by the golden rain are evident in visual images of the story produced throughout the 5th century. Such elements are already present on the earliest Attic depiction of Danae and the golden rain – a red-figure calyx crater by the Triptolemos Painter of ca. 490–480 B.C. (Fig. 1).[20] Here Danae is shown sitting on a kline, evidently her bed in her underground chamber of confinement. Her feet are supported by a footstool. Danae wears both a linen chiton with an overfold and an himation, which is draped over her upper legs. From the wall are suspended a mirror and a sakkos, that is a hairnet. Two rows of purple drops, signifying the golden rain, descend from the top of the pictorial field to Danae's lap. The virgin sits with knees pressed together but with chest thrown back and head tilted upwards as she holds onto the two ends of a fillet, which is wrapped around her head and looped over her gathered hair at the nape of her neck.

In recent scholarship, this image has been associated with representations of brides dressing for their wedding.

In accordance with this analogy, the activity Danae is engaged in has been understood as the binding of her hair with the fillet, in preparation for the maiden's "marriage" to Zeus.[21] Illustrations of Greek brides who are putting their hair up in their hairbands have been collected by Viktoria Sabetai.[22] Unquestionably, there are parallel features between such representations and Fig. 1. For example, the hair-binding bride in Fig. 2 sits on the edge of a kline with feet supported by a footstool, as does Danae in Fig. 1. Other depictions of brides dressing for their weddings include mirrors and hairnets, the attributes shown suspended from the wall in Danae's chamber.[23] Depicting Danae in the aspect of a bride would seem to imply that, like a willing bride, she consented to Zeus' amorous attentions. There is, however, one basic problem that impedes the immediate acceptance of this analogy for the scene on the calyx crater. Rather than preparing for her "wedding," Danae appears to be already experiencing its consummation, as is evident from the stream of golden rain, which apparently should be understood as Zeus' impregnating semen.[24]

A close examination of the figure of Danae reveals a related but slightly different possible interpretation; that is, Danae may be unbinding rather than binding her hair with the fillet. The fact that her hairnet has been put aside and is suspended from the wall would seem to support the idea that she is undressing rather than dressing. If engaged in this activity, Danae would still be following the role of

---

[19] Dow and Page, op. cit., vol. 2, p. 124.

[20] Calyx crater from Cerveteri in St. Petersburg, Hermitage Museum Б.1602 (637): J.-J. Maffre, "Danae," Lexicon Iconographicum Mythologiae Classicae (hereafter, LIMC), vol. 3, 1986, p. 327, no. 1, pl. 243. Recent publications of the crater are: Reeder, op. cit., p. 269–270; and K. Kilinski II, Greek Masculine Prowess in the Manifestations of Zeus, in Myth, Sexuality and Power: Images of Jupiter in Western Art, F. Van Keuren, ed., 1998, p. 34.

[21] See Viktoria Sabetai, The Washing Painter: A contribution to the wedding and genre iconography in the second half of the fifth century B.C., dissert. 1993, p. 37–40; and J. H. Oakley, Nuptial Nuances: Wedding Images in Non-Wedding Scenes of Myth, in E.D. Reeder et alii, Pandora: Women in Classical Greece, 1995, p. 68.

[22] Ibidem, p. 36–45. See also J.H. Oakley and R.H. Sinos, The Wedding in Ancient Athens, 1993, p. 17, figs. 21 and 23–27. Prof. Jenifer Neils offered the following observations in an email communication of February 23, 1999: "The tying of the hair also appears in sculpture. See Musée Calvet, Avignon, Silence et Fureur 1996 for examples [see the stelai in Avignon and from Rhamnous, figs. 33–34]. Also I think the girl next to Hera on the Parthenon E. frieze who is tying her hair is the bride Hebe; see my forthcoming article Reconfiguring the Gods on the Parthenon frieze, Art Bulletin, March 1999." For an illustration of this figure from the Parthenon frieze, see I. Jenkins, The Parthenon Frieze, 1994, p. 78, fig. V 28.

[23] See Oakley and Sinos, ibidem, p. 17–18, figs. 22 and 28.

a bride, but she would be like a bride in the thalamos, the bridal chamber, at the moment that the marriage is consummated. John H. Oakley and Rebecca H. Sinos have collected and illustrated Attic black-figure and red-figure depictions of the thalamos. In every example, the bridal bed (the kline) is present and emphasized, as in Fig. 1, but the consummation of the marriage is never depicted.[25] However, an activity on Danae's part of hair unbinding while Zeus' golden rain consummates the "marriage" can be understood as analogous to that of the undressing of the Greek bride, whose unveiling may have been performed by her husband in the bridal chamber.[26] The thesis that the bride's unveiling took place in the thalamos may perhaps find support in a 2nd-century B.C. terracotta group from Myrina, where a shy veiled girl (a bride?) sits on the edge of a kline next to a youthful male figure (a groom?), who puts his arm around the girl and appears to be in the process of successfully persuading her to consummate the marriage.[27] A Roman painting cycle from cubiculum D in the Villa under the Farnesina, Rome (dated ca. 19 B.C.), depicts a shy bride's transformation into a loving wife. In the first panel, the fully-clothed and veiled bride sits upright on the marriage bed, and pushes her

husband's hand off her thigh. In the second, she is undressed to the waist, and assertively pulls her husband's head towards her, as if attempting to kiss him. On the last panel, the happy couple lean against each other in a loose embrace, and turn their heads towards one another in a pose indicating they are about to kiss.[28]

Understanding Danae in Fig. 1 as unbinding her hair is consistent with the presence of the golden rain. It also provides a plausible explanation for Danae's pose. In illustrations on Attic red-figure vases that depict brides binding up their hair, as for example the pyxis by the Washing Painter dated ca. 420 B.C. (Fig. 2),[29] the bride bends her shoulders and head forward as she winds the fillet around her head and under her hair at the nape of her neck. She lifts her left arm and elbow up, and with her raised left hand, she pulls up the end of the fillet that is wrapped over her forehead. With her lowered right hand, she pulls the second fillet end that is wound around the hair at the nape of her neck forward and taut (see Fig. 3 for an attempt to replicate this pose). On this pyxis (Fig. 2), the bride appears to be about to twist the two fillet ends together and then wrap the conjoined ends over and around her hair, to create a bun. The pose of Danae on the calyx crater (Fig. 1) differs in one important respect – she holds both fillet ends loosely, with both elbows down. According to Mary Jones, hairdresser of Athens, Georgia, this is a posture that would only be possible for a woman who is taking her hair down. Ms. Jones also observed that the head can be positioned in a variety of inclinations while unbinding one's hair. However, the tilting of the head upwards, as with Danae on the calyx crater, is awkward, and seemed to her to signify a response of surprise at the sudden intrusion of the golden rain into her chamber (see Fig. 4 for an attempt to replicate Danae's pose in Fig. 1). To Ms. Jones, Danae in Fig. 1 seems to have been interrupted while in the process of taking her hair down, and has looked upwards in

[24] While Pherekydes describes Zeus as revealing his human form before having intercourse with Danae, other authors, including Asklepiades (who refers to Zeus as χρυσός), make no mention of the god's resumption of this shape after gaining entrance to Danae's chamber as the golden rain. See, for example, Sophocles, Antigone 950, where Danae is said to have "guarded a deposit of the seed of Zeus that had fallen in a golden rain" (Ζηνὸς ταμιεύεσκε γονὰς χρυσορύτους), trans. R. Jebb and P. Habel, web site www.perseus.tufts.edu; Pindar, Pythian 12.17, where Perseus is described as "born of free-flowing gold" (τὸν ἀπὸ χρυσοῦ...αὐτορύτου), trans. W.H. Race, 1997; and Isocrates, Helen 10.59, where it is stated that "as a shower of gold he [Zeus] united with Danae" (χρυσὸς...ῥυεὶς Δανάῃ), trans. G. Norlin, 1980.

[25] The Wedding in Ancient Athens, 1993, p. 35–37 and 41, figs. 100–114 and 129.

[26] See R. Rehm, Marriage to Death: The Conflation of Wedding and Funeral Rituals in Greek Tragedy, 1994, p. 141–142, for the view that the *anakalupteria* took place in the *thalamos* on the wedding night.

[27] R.A. Higgins, Greek Terracottas, 1967, p. 117, pl. pl. 54A; and J.J. Pollitt, Art in the Hellenistic Age, 1986, p. 134, fig. 147. Dr. Emma J. Stafford kindly called my attention to the statuette group, which is discussed in her forthcoming article, "Plutarch on Persuasion" (see note 53 below).

[28] John R. Clarke, Looking at Lovemaking: Constructions of Sexuality in Roman Art 100 B.C.–A.D. 250, 1998, p. 100–105, figs. 32–34. Prof. Brian E. McConnell very kindly called my attention to this recently-published book, and found a copy for me.

[29] The pyxis is from Athens and is at Würzburg, Universität Würzburg, Martin von Wagner Museum H 4455 (541). For the date of the pyxis and bibliography, see Sabetai, op. cit., p. 15; and Oakley and Sinos, op. cit., p. 17–18 and 134.

curiosity at the unexpected but not necessarily unwelcome intruder.

That this depiction of Danae should be understood as welcoming the golden rain, in agreement with Pherekydes' account, is reinforced by the receptive attitude of the maiden. As already pointed out, Danae not only tilts her head up as she gazes upwards at the falling golden rain; she also throws her chest back, in an open posture that may signify her enjoyment of the sudden intrusion.[30] Furthermore, the way in which she tugs at the ends of her fillet may signify both the action of taking her hairband off, and her experience of sexual pleasure as the golden rain pours onto her lap. Taking all these features into account – that is the bridal references, hair unbinding and receptive posture – it appears that rather than being raped, Danae in Fig. 1 is consenting to and possibly even enjoying her strange union with the most potent of Greek gods.

Contemporary and later 5th-century illustrations of Danae receiving the golden rain express Danae's eagerness to take up the golden rain more blatantly. A fragment of an unpublished Attic red-figure cup from the sanctuary of Artemis at Brauron is known through its published description. Dated ca. 490–480 B.C., i.e. in the same decade as Fig. 1, Danae sits in a similar posture with her feet resting on a footstool and her chest thrown back. On this fragment attributed to the Brygos Painter, Danae wears only a linen chiton; her discarded himation has possibly been recognized as suspended on the left, while on the right is a mirror. She is said to have "les cheveux noués," that is her hair is still bound. According to the description, she holds up the overfold of her chiton in order to catch the golden rain, while looking upwards at it.[31]

On a fragment of a red-figure cup of ca. 480–470 B.C., an incompletely-preserved Danae sits on the edge of a kline while looking up at the falling golden rain and extending her forearms under it, as if in an attempt to catch it.[32] A better-preserved Danae on an Attic white-ground lekythos from about 460–450 B.C. (Fig. 5) is engaged in the same acitivity – that is, she tries to catch the golden rain in her forearms. Here, unlike any other Attic vase illustrating the same theme, Danae sits on a type of backless seat called a diphros, and the confined space in her chamber is emphasized by the two columns that sandwich her between them. The meander border over her head, evidently signaling the position of the roof of her chamber, comes so close to her head that she must look to the side, rather than up at the golden rain.[33]

Danae on a slightly earlier Attic red-figure lekythos by the Painter of the Yale Lekythos, dated ca. 470–460 B.C., eagerly extends her arms out in front of her and captures the falling golden rain more successfully in her draped arms, which are covered with the long sleeves of her chiton. She sits on a klismos, the chair with a curved back, with her himation wrapped around her waist and legs. As in Fig. 1, a hairnet and mirror are suspended from the wall. However, unlike Fig. 1, Danae has already let her hair down; for although a fillet is still wrapped around her head, her loosened hair falls on her back. A wool basket is on the ground next to her knees, an attribute signifying housewifely work and virtue that is frequently among the gifts presented to brides.[34]

On an Attic red-figure hydria from Greece, dated ca. 440–430 B.C., Danae sits on the edge of her kline with bare feet dangling and collects the golden rain in her himation, which is draped over both her arms. Her posture is upright, unlike the backwards lean of Danae in Fig. 1. However, that the image is intended to be erotic is under-

---

[30] Cf. Anthony Milton Anninos, Danae: a comparative study in artistic approaches to a myth, M.A. thesis, Berkeley, 1977, p. 13: "Most likely the Triptolemos Painter had portrayed Danae, on her couch, fully clothed in order to mitigate the element of eroticism. That he was not averse to depicting nude women and explicit sexual acts is shown by a vase of his in Tarquinia (ARV² p. 367, no. 93)."

[31] Cup fragment in Brauron Museum: LIMC, vol. 3, p. 327, no. 2. Here Danae is said to "recueillir dans son giron [sc. la pluie d'or] en relevant l'apoptygma de son chiton." According to an email communcation from Prof. John H. Oakley of February 24, 1999, "Lilly Kahil's publication of this material [from Brauron] is on line to be published by the Greek Archaeological Society or TAPA."

[32] Cup fragment from Athens in Athens, storerooms of IIIrd Ephoreia, 0.75: LIMC, vol. 3, p. 327, no. 3; J.-J. Maffre, Une nouvelle représentation de Danaé recevant la pluie d'or, Studien zur Mythologie und Vasenmalerei: Konrad Schauenburg, 1986, p. 71–74, pl. 11.1.

[33] Corinth, Museum MP 90: J.H. Oakley, Zwei alte Vasen – Zwei neue Danaebilder, Archäologischer Anzeiger 1990, p. 65–69.

[34] Athens, National Museum 17640: LIMC, vol. 3, p. 327, no. 4; S. Karusu, Die "Schutzflehende" Barberini, Antike Kunst 13, 1970, p. 36, fig. 2. On the *kalathos*, or wool basket, see Oakley and Sinos, op. cit., p. 38–39, figs. 29 and 117.

scored by the presence of Eros – this is the first example to include the god, who hovers in the air behind Danae, with his torso bent towards the maiden, as he holds out a white fillet in both hands.[35] Danae's hair does not fall loose on her shoulders, but appears to be up in a bun.

Danae's interest in the golden rain is again made manifest on an Attic red-figure kalpis-hydria of ca. 430–420 B.C. (Fig. 6). Here she catches the golden rain in a pouch that she creates by holding up part of her himation with both hands. She gazes up at the descending rain while she sits on her kline in a casual, slouching posture, with the feet of her crossed legs supported by a footstool or low table. Her hair is bound up in a fillet, and a mirror is suspended from the wall. Danae's enraptured concentration on the collecting of the rain is contrasted with the excited gestures of Hermes, who has evidently shown Zeus the location of the fair maiden's underground chamber, and the female attendant, believed to be Danae's nurse.[36]

A statue type of ca. 430–410 B.C., of which the most famous copy is called the Barberini Suppliant, may introduce a more erotically-charged image of Danae. This figure of problematic interpretation sits on a low base that has been identified as a chest. She gazes upwards while leaning back on her left arm and raising her right forearm. Her chiton has fallen off her left shoulder to reveal her left breast, and one sandal has fallen off. The baring of a breast and the absence of a sandal have been interpreted as erotic motifs which are consistent with the welcoming attitude that Pherekydes ascribes to Danae. Furthermore, two aspects of the figure's pose – the way in which she leans backwards and raises her right forearm, have been seen in earlier depictions of the Danae myth. Yet a number of scholars have hesitated to identify the figure as Danae, claiming that her unsmiling expression denotes a mood of

sadness. However, rather than feeling sadness she may instead be experiencing a glow of pleasure as Zeus' warm golden rain flows over her body.[37]

If the Barberini Suppliant has correctly been identified as Danae, then the influence of this statuary type may be evident on contemporary and later depictions of Zeus' mistress. For example, Danae on a contemporary Boeotian red-figure bell crater of ca. 430–410 B.C. (Fig. 7) has a pose that is similar to the statue – here also she leans back on her left arm, raises her right forearm and looks up at the descending golden rain. Now rather than having just one breast bare, both her ample breasts and her stomach are revealed, as the large, round raindrops fall on her nude flesh. The inscription next to her head confirms that she is Danae, although the vase was manufactured at Thebes, home of Alkmene, another mistress of Zeus.[38]

A contemporary and compositionally-similar Boeotian red-figure bell crater, although uninscribed, has been identified as another depiction of a bare-breasted Danae.[39] However, as A.D. Ure has observed, this lady "is a queenly figure, adorned with jewels, receiving with poise and dignity the manifestation of the love of Zeus. The Louvre krater (Fig. 7), though plainly deriving from the same source, shows an untidy, rather pert young woman with something of the air of a maid impersonating her mistress."[40] One difference that Ure did not call attention to is the way the particles above the chest of the bare-breasted lady are arranged. Instead of falling in a vertical stream, as in Fig. 7, they are bunched together in an inverted triangle at the top of the panel. One wonders if

---

[35] Hydria, Adolphseck 38: LIMC, vol. 3, p. 327, no. 5, pl. 243; and CVA Schloss Fasanerie (Adolphseck) vol. 1, p. 19, pl. 29.3, where the description is given: "Auf die Frau fliegt ein Eros zu, der in der ausgestreckten Händen eine weiß gemalte Binde hält." For a fragment of an Attic red-figure pyxis lid from the late 5th century that shows Eros in front of Danae who captures the golden rain in her drapery, see Oakley, *Zwei alte Vasen*, cit. in note 33, p. 69–70, figs. 5–6.

[36] Kalpis-hydria, Boston, Museum of Fine Arts 68.18: LIMC, vol. 3, p. 327, no. 6; C.C. Vermeule, Recent Museum Acquisitions, *Burlington Magazine* 112, Jan.–Dec. 1970, p. 628, figs. 100 and 102; and Oakley, *Zwei alte Vasen*, op. cit., p. 68, fig. 4.

[37] Marble statue, Paris, Louvre 3433: Beth Cohen, Divesting the Female Breast of Clothes in Classical Sculpture, in *Naked Truths: Women, sexuality and gender in classical art and archaeology*, A.O. Koloski-Ostrow and C.L. Lyons, eds., 1997, p. 66–67 and 79–82, fig. 3; J. Boardman, *Greek Sculpture: The Classical Period: A Handbook*, 1985, fig. 221; K. Schefold, *Die Göttersage in der klassischen und hellenistischen Kunst*, 1981, p. 240–241, fig. 239; LIMC, vol. 3, p. 330–331, no. 40, and p. 335; and S. Karusu, Die "Schutzflehende" Barberini, *Antike Kunst* 13, 1970, p. 34–47, pl. 22.

[38] Crater, Paris, Louvre CA 925: LIMC, vol. 3, p. 328, no. 9, pl. 244; and A.D. Ure, Boeotian Vases with Women's Heads, *American Journal of Archaeology* 57, 1953, p. 246–247 and 249 and pl. 67.7.

[39] Crater, Athens, Nat. Mus. 12593: LIMC, vol. 3, p. 327–328, no. 8, pl. 244.

[40] Ure, ibidem, p. 247.

Zeus' encounter with Alkmene rather than Danae may be depicted on this second bell crater, with a scheme that was borrowed from Danae images like Fig. 7. According to the Boeotian poet Pindar, Zeus visited Alkmene as well as Danae metamorphosed into gold; but in this case the golden form he assumed was snow rather than rain.[41] Thus, the triangle of particles above the maiden's chest may be a snow cloud.[42]

As the foregoing survey indicates, 5th-century depictions of Danae and one possible representation of Alkmene all seem to express in a subtle or blatant fashion a sexually receptive attitude on the part of Zeus' mistress(es).[43] Judging from the fact that no Attic vase-painter is known to have been female,[44] the determination that Danae's response to Zeus' amorous attentions was positive probably represents a male point of view. Furthermore, since the 5th-century depictions of Danae are replete with activities and articles befitting a bride, it may be suggested that Danae's welcoming behavior was considered a model for brides at the moment their marriage was consummated, and in subsequent sexual unions with their husbands. Surely such a welcoming and accepting attitude on the part of brides would have been advantageous to grooms, who would thereby have been assured that their sexually-inexperienced virgin brides would cooperate in initial love-making activities. Different genres of literary evidence, presumably all by male authors, support this analogy of Danae behaving like an ideal bride – surviving Hippocratic writings, other medical literature, anecdotes from ancient history, and treatises on love and marriage.

That women of good character like Danae were conceived of by the Greeks as having the capacity to enjoy sexual experiences is already borne out by early literary sources; the most memorable is the fragment attributed to Hesiod's Melampodia, in which the seer Teiresias, who had lived both as a man and a woman, delivered the judgment to Zeus and Hera that women derived ten times the pleasure from sexual intercourse as men.[45]

Significantly, in Hippocratic writings, female sexual pleasure was considered necessary for conception. Female pleasure was required, because it was believed that, like the male, the female released seed. Since the male was observed to release his seed at the height of his sexual excitement, a belief arose that the same held true for the female. If properly aroused sexually, the female was thought to release her seed when stimulated by the male's ejaculation of his seed. This sequence is poetically expressed in chapter 4

[41] Pindar, Isthmian 7.5–10.

[42] For the theory that Athens 12593 depicts Zeus visiting Alkmene, see J. Boardman, J. Dörig, W. Fuchs and M. Hirmer, The Art and Architecture of Ancient Greece, 1967, p. 362–363, fig. 159.

[43] Cf. the conclusions of Nina Maria Christensen, The Myth of Danae in Pompeian Domestic Painting, M.A. thesis, Univ. of California, Riverside, 1997, p. 49: "From the visual evidence, there is no indication of a struggle. Instead, as seen in the House of Regina Margherita, an example which continues and expands upon the Greek formula, Danae participates willingly by opening her *himation* to receive the golden shower. Moreover, with the appearance in the paintings from Pompeii of Cupid in the Caccia Antica example, Jupiter in his anthropomorphic form in both the Regina Margherita and Gavius Rufus examples and Danae's *strophium* in the Regina Margherita example, the image begins to take on the character of a romantic image."

[44] The one possible exception to the norm that Attic vase-painters were male is the scene on an Attic red-figure hydria by the Leningrad Painter in Milan, the Torno Collection, C 278. On this vase, found in a woman's grave at Ruvo, three beardless youths and a single woman are shown working with brushes on vessels in a workshop. The problem with interpreting this depiction is that the vases the male and female workers are toiling over may be metal and not ceramic. On this depiction, see M.S. Venit, "The Caputi Hydria and Working Women in Classical Athens," Classical World 81, 1988, p. 265–272, figs. 1–2; R. Green, The Caputi Hydria, Journal of Hellenic Studies 81, 1961, p. 73–75, pls. 6–7; François Lissarrague, Figures of Women, in A History of Women in the West: I. From Ancient Goddesses to Christian Saints, P.S. Pantel, ed., and A. Goldhammer, trans., 1992, p. 207–208, fig. 45; D.C. Kurtz, ed., Greek Vases: Lectures by J.D. Beazley, 1989, p. 43–44; J.V. Noble, The Techniques of Painted Attic Pottery, rev. ed., 1988, figs. 2 and 206; and G.M.A. Richter, The Craft of Athenian Pottery, 1923, p. 70–71, fig. 66. Prof. John H. Oakley pointed out to me the need to bring up the issue of the masculine gender of Attic vase-painters, and kindly provided some of the references to the Milan hydria; Prof. Jenifer Neils generously provided other references.

[45] For the text and an English translation of the fragment, see Hesiod: The Homeric Hymns and Homerica, H. G. Evelyn-White, trans., 1914, p. 268–269, frg. 3. For a general discussion of the myth, see N. Loraux, The Experiences of Tiresias, P. Wissing, trans., 1995, p. 10–12. Cf. Xenophon, Symposium 8.21, on female pleasure in intercourse. See also Clarke, op. cit., p. 49: "It is likely that the myth of Tiresias expresses the classical Greek male's construction of woman: she lives for sex and finds it more pleasurable than a man does."

of the Hippocratic work called On the Seed, as translated by Iain M. Lonie:

> Both the pleasure and the heat [of the woman] reach their peak simultaneously with the arrival of the [man's] sperm in the womb, and then they cease. If, for example, you pour wine on a flame, first of all the flame flares up and increases for a short period when you pour the wine on, then it dies away. In the same way the woman's heat flares up in response to the man's sperm, and then dies away.[46]

Another Hippocratic work called Regimen I emphasizes the need for simultaneous emission of the male and female seeds:

> Growth belongs, not only to the man's secretion, but also to that of the woman…When it happens that both are emitted together to one place, they conjoin, the fire to the fire and the water likewise…On one day in each month it can solidify, and master the advancing parts, and that only if it happen that parts are emitted from both parents together in one place.[47]

The History of Animals reiterates the need for both sexual partners to achieve ecstasy at the same moment:

> Failure to keep pace with others brings failure to generate…For if it is true that the wife too contributes to the seed and the generation, plainly there is need of equal speed on both sides.[48]

This medical linking of successful conception to simultaneous orgasm by both partners in love-making appears to represent one commonly-held Greek belief concerning reproduction. Such a belief would certainly have affected the way fifth-century Athenian men viewed marital sex. For pleasuring their wives would not be considered to simply be the happy result of a sexually fulfilling marriage; it would also have been viewed as necessary to insure legitimate citizen offspring.[49]

One predominant trend in recent scholarship has made claims implying that "ancient Greek men had little physical interest in their wives." This summary quote comes from Mary Lefkowitz's article, "Wives and Husbands," that was recently published in the volume Women in Antiquity.[50] Lefkowitz disputes such claims, insisting that married couples could feel "strong ties of affection…, and even sexual attraction."[51] To arrive at an idea of what constituted the ideal ancient marriage, she looks at passages from fragmentary and whole dramas, as well as affectionate honorific funerary inscriptions.[52]

Evidence indicating that mutual sexual attraction was possible in marriage and heterosexual relationships can also be found in Plutarch, who quotes many earlier literary sources, and in Herodotos. The character representing Plutarch himself in Plutarch's Dialogue on Love makes the following positive observations regarding the benefits of sex in marriage:

> In the case of lawful wives, physical union is the beginning of friendship, a sharing, as it were, in great mysteries. Pleasure is short; but the respect and kindness and mutual affection and loyalty that daily spring from it convicts neither the Delphians of raving when they call Aphrodite 'Harmony' nor Homer when he designates such a union as 'friendship.' It also proves that Solon was a very experienced legislator of marriage laws. He prescribed that a man should consort with his wife not less than three times a month – not for

---

[46] Quoted by Lesley Dean-Jones, The Politics of Pleasure: Female Sexual Appetite in the Hippocratic Corpus, in Discourses in Sexuality: From Aristotle to Aids, 1992, p. 69; from The Hippocratic Treatises On Generation, On the Nature of the Child, Diseases IV, I.M. Lonie, comment., 1981, 4.2, p. 2–3. For another translation of the same passage, see Hippocrates On Intercourse and Pregnancy, T.U.H. Ellinger, trans., 1952, p. 28–29. For the Greek text of this passage, see Hippocrate, vol. 11, R. Joly, ed. and trans. (in French), 1970, De la génération 4.2, p. 47. For commentary on this passage and quotations from additional Greek authors who believed in the release of female seed, see Lonie, ibidem, p. 119–121; and Sarah George, Human Conception and Fetal Growth: A Study in the Development of Greek Thought from the Presocratics through Aristotle, dissert. 1982, p. 1–2 and 34–123.

[47] Hippocrates, vol. 4, W.H.S. Jones, trans., 1931, Regimen I.27, p. 265 and 267.

[48] Aristotle, History of Animals, Books VII–X, D.M. Balme, trans., 1991, X.5, 636b, p. 507 and 509.

[49] Cf. Andrew Stewart, Reflections, in Sexuality in Ancient Art, Natalie Boymel Kampen, ed., 1996, p. 148–150, who only accepts this view for 4th century B.C. and later Greek males.

[50] Ed. by Ian McAuslan and Peter Walcot, Greece and Rome Studies, 3, 1996, p. 72.

[51] Ibidem.

[52] Ibidem., pp. 67–82.

pleasure surely, but as cities renew their mutual agreements from time to time, just so he must have wished this to be a renewal of marriage and with such an act of tenderness to wipe out the complaints that accumulate from everyday living.[53]

In the same dialogue, this same character representing Plutarch makes these positive comments regarding sex in marriage:

For intercourse without Eros is like hunger and thirst, which can be sated, but never achieve a noble end. It is by means of Eros that the goddess removes the cloying effect of pleasure and creates affection and fusion. That is the reason Parmenides declares that Eros is the most ancient work of Aphrodite; his words in the Cosmogony are:

And first of all the gods she framed was Love.

But Hesiod [Theogony 120], in my opinion, was more scientific when he depicted Eros as the first-born of them all, in order to make him indispensable for the generation of all things.[54]

Later on in the same dialogue the character of Plutarch observes:

Doesn't Love change the ill-tempered and sullen and make them more sociable and agreeable?

When hearth's ablaze, a house appears more cheerful;

likewise a man seems to become more radiant through the heat of love.[55]

Female desire does not go unmentioned by Plutarch. In the same dialogue the character representing Plutarch quotes Aeschylus as being correct when the tragedian observed:

An ardent eye betrays the tender girl
Who once has tasted of the joys of love.[56]

Herodotos makes reference to female expression of sexuality in the tale relating how Lydian Gyges objects to King Candaules' wish that Gyges view his wife naked:

"Master," he said, "what an unsound suggestion, that I should see my mistress naked! When a woman's clothes come off, she dispenses with her modesty, too."[57]

The foregoing quotes provide some indication of the nature and extent of the literary evidence supporting the thesis that mutually pleasurable sex in marriage was considered desirable by the ancient Greeks.

A final observation brings us back to visual representations of Danae and the golden rain that are illustrated in Figs. 1, 5–7 and elsewhere. Strangely, these 5th-century depictions of Danae conceiving Perseus have been largely ignored in scholarly discussions of female sexual response to the amorous attentions of the gods. Instead, pursuit and abduction scenes such as Fig. 8 have been examined,[58] especially in the articles by Andrew Stewart,[59] Christiane Sourvinou-Inwood,[60] and Ada Cohen.[61] In his article, Stewart observes that such representations were "produced by and mainly for men in the context of the symposium."[62] According to Stewart's perception, these pursuit and abduction scenes related to "a prime theme of the symposium," which was "discourse about sex."[63]

---

53 Plutarch's Moralia, vol. 9, trans. E.L. Minar, F.H. Sandbach and W.C. Helmbold, 1961, Erotikos 769A–B, p. 427. Dr. Emma J. Stafford, University of Wales, Lampeter, called my attention to Plutarch's Dialogue on Love, which she cites in her forthcoming essay, "Plutarch on Persuasion," to appear this year (1999) in Plutarch's Advice to the bride and groom, and A consolation to his wife: English translation, commentary, interpretive essays, and bibliography, Sarah B. Pomeroy, ed.

54 Ibidem, 756E–F, p. 351.

55 Ibidem, 762D, p. 387.

56 Ibidem, 767C, p. 417.

57 Herodotos 1.8, A.D. Godley and S. Ott, trans., web site www.perseus.tufts.edu.

58 The most important general study of this type of scene is S. Kaempf-Dimitriadou, Die Liebe der Götter in der attischen Kunst des 5. Jahrhunderts v. Chr., 1979. Fig. 8, an Attic red-figure neck-amphora by the Harrow Painter, ca. 490–480 B.C., is at Oxford, University of Mississippi, University Museums: Kaempf-Dimitriadou, p. 101, no. 305; and John Stephenson, in Jupiter's Loves and his Children, F. Van Keuren, curator, 1997, p. 45–46.

59 Rape?, in Ellen D. Reeder et alii, Pandora: Women in Classical Greece, 1995, p. 74–90.

60 A Series of Erotic Pursuits: Images and Meanings, Journal of Hellenic Studies 107, 1987, p. 131–157.

61 Portrayals of Abduction in Greek Art: Rape or Metaphor?, in Sexuality in Ancient Art: Near East, Egypt, Greece, and Italy, Natalie Boymel Kampen, ed., 1996, p. 117–135.

62 Rape?, cit. in note 59, p. 74.

These scenes, suggests Stewart, promoted "the cause of Athenian masculine self-assertion," by expressing "male dominance over unwilling females;"[64] at the same time that the pursued women on the vases are controlled by the men, "these pictures stress female resistance."[65]

One wonders if Stewart might be misconstruing the type of control that heroes and gods were believed to exert over the objects of their affection. Might they be exerting control through persuasion rather than force? Might the heroines be hesitating rather than resisting? Mary Lefkowitz pointed out that "there is emphasis on the persuasive power of the god's glance; the woman moves away from him but looks back, as if drawn to him."[66] In Fig. 8, Ariadne gazes into the eyes of Dionysos, her divine husband-to-be, while not seeming to resist his gentle touch on her right shoulder. Yet at the same time that she turns her head back to look at her stately pursuer, her feet and body are directed away from him.

Images of Danae have much in common with such pursuit scenes. The period of production of the Athenian and Boeotian vases with Danae that we have examined (Figs. 1 and 5–7) parallels the era when divine pursuits are attested on Athenian vases, that is from 500 to 400 B.C.[67] Furthermore, that at least some images of Danae were intended for display at the symposium is demonstrated by their presence on craters, the vessels used at the symposium to dilute wine with water (see Figs. 1 and 7). Depictions of Danae show a moment that can be considered to be a narrative sequel to mythological pursuit scenes. Here, the pursuit is over, and sexual intercourse has begun. Clearly Zeus does not take the virgin by force. As he pours into Danae's chamber in the abstract and non-threatening form of golden rain, Danae does not turn away. Instead, as has been demonstrated, she welcomes the fertilizing liquid,[68] appearing to take pleasure in its warm flow over her draped or undraped body (Figs. 1 and 7); or she seems to enjoy capturing it in her arms or drapery (Figs. 5 and 6).

One can imagine that to a Greek male viewer, especially a participant in a symposium, the sexually-receptive attitudes that Danae adopts would have been considered ideal. Like the character of Chaerea in Terence's Eunuch, such a viewer may have hoped to imitate Zeus in assuming the form of golden rain, and being welcomed to the bosom of his beloved.[69] The female viewer,[70] on the other hand, would probably have identified with Danae's experience. With Zeus' presence downplayed pictorially, as in the lekythos in Fig. 5 where he is a single vertical stripe of drops, an ancient female viewer could easily have imagined Danae's loneliness in her chamber of confinement, as well as her positive response to the miraculous visitation of the golden rain to her loveless chamber.

In short, regardless of which gender an ancient viewer happened to be, he or she would probably have considered vase-paintings of Danae receiving the golden rain to be depictions of a pleasurable female experience. If this hypothesis is correct, it is difficult to maintain that a completely different type of narrative sequel – sexual assault against the will of the pursued women – was implied by scenes of the gods in amorous pursuit.

---

[63] Ibidem, p. 86.

[64] Ibidem.

[65] Ibidem.

[66] Seduction and Rape in Greek Myth, cit. in note 8, p. 22.

[67] Rape?, cit. in note 59, chart 1, p. 87

[68] For the theory that "the original significance of Danae and her golden shower" was "a mythical expression whereby the sky-god fertilises the earth", see A.B. Cook, Zeus: A Study in Ancient Religion, vol. 3.1, 1940, p. 473–478.

[69] Cf. lines 583 ff., trans. J. Sargeaunt, 1912.

> The girl sat in the room looking at a picture on the wall. The subject was the story of Jove's sending down a shower of gold into Danae's bosom. I fell to gazing at it too, and the fact that he had played a like game long ago made me exult all the more, a god's turning himself into a man and stealing on to another man's roof-tiles and a woman's being fooled by means of a shower, and what a god too! He 'whose thunder shakes the highest realms of heaven.' Was I, a mere manikin, not to imitate him? Imitate I would, and like nothing better.

[70] For a discussion that suggests distinctive male and female viewers' responses to the erotic cycle in apodyterium 7 of the Suburban Baths, Pompeii (dated 62–79 A.D.), see Clarke, cit. in note 28, p. 212–240 and 278, pls. 9–16.

**Fig. 1A.** Attic red-figure calyx crater by the Triptolemos Painter, ca. 490–480 B.C.; Danae and the golden rain. St. Petersburg, Hermitage Museum Б. 1602 (637). Photo courtesy of the Museum.

**Fig. 1B.** Attic red-figure calyx crater by the Triptolemos Painter, ca. 490–480 B.C.; Danae and the golden rain. St. Petersburg, Hermitage Museum 637. Drawing from E. Gerhard, *Danae: Ein griechisches Vasenbild*, 1854.

**Fig. 2.** Attic red-figure pyxis from Athens by the Washing Painter, ca. 420 B.C.; bride binding her hair. Würzburg, Universität Würzburg, Martin von Wagner Museum H 4455 (541). Photo by K. Oehrlein.

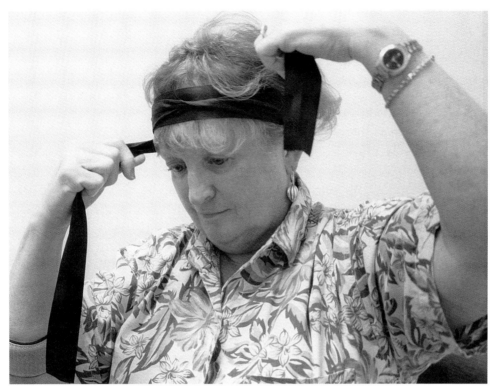

**Fig. 3.** Mary Jones, hairdresser of Athens, Georgia, binding her hair as in Fig. 2. Photo by the author.

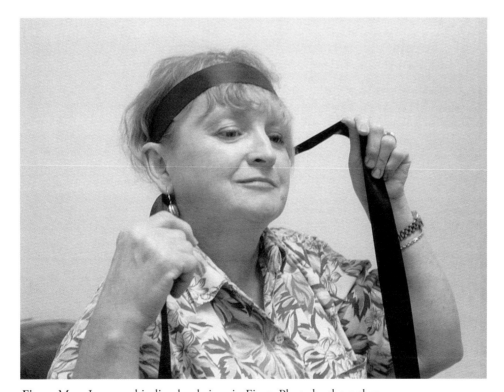

**Fig. 4.** Mary Jones, unbinding her hair as in Fig. 1. Photo by the author.

**Fig. 5.** Attic white-ground lekythos, ca. 460–450 B.C.; Danae and
the golden rain. Corinth, Museum MP 90. Photo courtesy of the
American School of Classical Studies, Corinth Excavations,
I. Ioannidou and L. Bartziotou.

**Fig. 6.** Attic red-figure kalpis-hydria, ca. 430–420 B.C.; Danae and the golden rain, Hermes and Danae's nurse?. Boston, Museum of Fine Arts 68.18, Otis Norcross Fund. Photo courtesy of the Museum.

**Fig. 7.** Boeotian red-figure bell crater from Boeotia, ca. 430–410 B.C.; Danae and the golden rain. Paris, Louvre CA 925. Photo M. and P. Chuzeville.

**Fig. 8.** Attic red-figure neck-amphora by the Harrow Painter, ca. 490–480 B.C.; Dionysos and Ariadne. Oxford, University of Mississippi, University Museums, David M.
Robinson Memorial Collection 1977.3.87 a-b, gift of Mr. and Mrs. Frank S. Peddle Jr.,
1961. Photo courtesy of the Museum.

# CITYSCAPE IN THE ROMAN WORLD

*Brian E. McConnell*

Today we think of cities in terms of a recognizable skyline. It is common to find maps with axonometric projections of topographic features – mountains, valleys and lakes are shown in three-dimensional illusion along with cities which are identified as clusters of buildings.[1] If we look closely at those building-clusters we see that they consist of certain famous monuments and an outline of the cluster as a whole (Fig. 1). How we view the urban skyline and recognize the city which it represents, how we recognize symbolic representations of a city through its form, or cityscape,[2] are very similar to how we read words. Psychologists and linguists have long debated the precise process which goes on when we read – do we recognize a string of letters or do we read whole words (Fig. 2)? What helps us accelerate this process when we speed-read? The consensus of opinion seems to rest somewhere between the recognition of single letters and whole words – we narrow down the lexical possibilities by identifying the first letter of a word and perhaps a few prominent characters in the middle and anticipate the meaning from the length and shape which the word seems to have; the context of the sentence confirms our anticipation.[3] And all of this takes place in fractions of a second!

The parallel between reading words and recognizing architectural ensembles can be seen in the identification of specific famous buildings or monuments which correspond to prominent letters, and then in the identification of the silhouette of the city skyline as a whole which corresponds to the length and shape of the word. Studies in urban development show that the relationship between individual buildings, the sky, and the architectural whole was very much on the minds of those who were developing the first architectural skylines in the United States.[4] In Boston, an 1892 ordinance limiting the first skyscrapers to a height of 125 feet beyond which only steeples, domes, towers or cupolas could be erected for strictly ornamental purpose was aimed at preserving the so-called 'sacred skyline.'[5]

Although this urban aesthetic would seem to be a phenomenon of our own modern era, it was present also in antiquity and became a characteristic particularly of Roman art.[6] The representation of a city as an architectural ensemble in the Roman world is very different from the kind of allegorical representations of cities which were common among the Greeks[7] precisely because it requires a degree of coherence among several structures in order to produce a recognizable form. First by looking at the Ro-

---

[1] As an example of this kind of map, see the Unique Media Maps of various locations in North America.

[2] J.G. Links, Townscape Painting and Drawing, 1972, p. 1, offers a general definition for the term 'cityscape': "Cityscape can be broadly defined to include anything from a detailed overview of an entire city to a close-up portrayal of a few buildings, but it is always concerned with some ensemble of man-made structures and spaces and often includes the presence of some natural topographical feature."

[3] L. Henderson, Orthography and Word Recognition in Reading, 1982, p. 231–236; D. Besner, E. Davelaar, D. Alcott, and P. Parry, Wholistic Reading of Alphabetic Print: Evidence from the FDM and the FBI, in L. Henderson ed, Orthographies and Reading, 1984, p. 121–135. The exception to the rule – when words are written entirely in capital letters seems to prove the point – don't you slow down when you read an inscription on a building?

[4] The term 'cityscape' is said to have originated as an Americanism in 1850, while the term 'skyline', which had been simply a synonym for 'horizon', came to mean a collection of buildings in 1896 (Bill Bryson, Made in America: an informal history of the English language in the United States, 1994, p. 98, but without further specification).

[5] Michael Holleran and Robert Fogelson, The Sacred Skyline: Boston's Opposition to the Skyscraper 1891–1928, MIT Center for Real Estate Development Working Paper #9, August 1987, p. 30–49. Only in 1916 when the concept of zoning was introduced creating a restricted area downtown where construction could exceed the 125-foot limit did people begin to see the skyscrapers of center-city as a true symbol of Boston. The authors make the significant point that while the slender forms of church spires tend to separate individual buildings along the urban horizon, the block-like masses of skyscrapers tend to create a visual tectonic whole.

man Forum we shall see that Rome's city center did have a skyline profile; then we shall focus our attention upon one building which seems to be a key to that profile – the so-called Tabularium. The origins of this building type lie within landscape architecture of the Hellenistic world of the Aegean and Italy, yet its place is unique in the development of the urban landscape of Republican Rome. Building ensembles shown in skyline profile begin to appear in Roman art following the appearance of the late Hellenistic architectural innovation represented by the so-called Tabularium.[8] As a result of this innovation, the Romans and their successors would never see the city in the same way.[9]

The so-called Tabularium has for centuries been identified as the structure which extends some 74 meters across a saddle in the Capitoline hill between the Temple of Jupiter Optimus Maximus and the Arx with its Temple of Juno Moneta.[10] Unlike the two temples which were set upon the space they occupied, this building filled its space and adapted itself to the irregular form between the Clivus Capitolinus, the street on its southwestern side, and the Gradus Monetae (later the Scalae Gemoniae), a stairway leading from the Roman Forum to the Arx on the building's northeastern side. To a great extent the so-called Tabularium also establishes a continuum between the two independent religious structures.

The Roman building is little preserved beyond its foundations. Richard Delbrueck, in his *Hellenistische Bauten in Latium* of 1907, carefully examined the details of the structure.[11] The building is hidden beneath Mich-

elangelo's Palazzo Senatorio, but we can see that the portion on the southern, or Forum, side still rests on a supporting wall in ashlar masonry. Above this supporting wall there were at least two covered walkways. The lower is still preserved, and it was an arcade open on the Forum side by a series of eleven archways each five meters wide and ten meters high and flanked on the exterior by Doric half-columns. The upper walkway may have been a true portico with a Corinthian colonnade in Travertine marble. Architectural elements from the colonnade include a fragment of a capital, a fragment of a geison with dentil

[6] The notion of Urban Aesthetic is one of the favorite themes of R. Ross Holloway, and it is the pleasure of this author to acknowledge his debt to Prof. Holloway for introducing him to it. This paper has benefited from presentation in one form or another at Brandeis University, Emory University, and De Pauw University and from research materials found particularly in the libraries of Columbia University, the University of Michigan, Ann Arbor, and the University of Georgia. The author would also like to thank Prof. F. Van Keuren of the University of Georgia for her helpful comments in its preparation.

[7] R. Hincks, *Myth and Allegory in Ancient Art*, 1939, p. 67–76 describes Greek representations of cities as appearing in three more or less separate stages: 1) as a guardian divinity or eponymous founder, 2) as an allegorical figure with emblematic attributes, 3) as the tyche of the particular place. Together these stages show a progressive abstraction from definite personalities to pure, allegorical concepts.

[8] It is appropriate to use the words 'so-called' to qualify the name 'Tabularium' because of a further challenge to its traditional identification. Nicholas Purcell (Atrium Libertatis, Papers of the British School at Rome, 61, 1993, p. 125–155. The Author wishes to thank N. Purcell, as well as F. Millar of Brasenose College, Oxford University, for an advance copy of this article.) has proposed that the Roman building beneath the Palazzo Senatorio was not the Tabularium but the Atrium Libertatis mentioned by Cicero in a letter to his brother-in-law Atticus dating to 54 B.C (Ad. Att. IV.16.8, trans. D.R. Shackleton Bailey):

> "Paulus has now almost roofed his basilica in the middle of the Forum, using the original antique pillars. The other one, which he gave out on contract, he is constructing in magnificent style. It is indeed a most admired and glorious edifice. So Caesar's friends (I mean Oppius and myself, choke at that if you must) have thought nothing of spending sixty million sesterces on the work which you used to be so enthusiastic about, to widen the Forum and extend it as far as the Hall of Liberty (Atrium Libertatis). We couldn't settle with the previous owners for a smaller sum. We shall achieve something really glorious."

Purcell points out the fact that no other town in Italy is known to have had a records archive so large, nor do the preserved rooms fit the kind of records facilities one finds at the southern end of the forum at Pompeii.

Roger Ulrich, Julius Caesar and the Creation of the Forum Iulium, American Journal of Archaeology 97, 1993, p. 49–80), on the other hand, has pointed to the ambiguity in the passage from Cicero's letter to Atticus regarding the building project of 54 B.C. Although he believes that the expansion of the Forum refers to work to the north, in the area which would become the Forum of Julius Caesar, he does not believe that the work in 54 B.C. was for the Forum so conceived; rather, he envisions a more loosely arranged set of buildings one of which replaced the Atrium Libertatis which he locates on the spot of the later Temple of Venus Genetrix. Only after 48 B.C. was the Forum of Julius Caesar designed as we know it today, using the Temple of Concord as an architectural antecedent for the Temple of Venus Genetrix.

and egg-and-dart moulding, elements of at least two columns, and the corner block of a frieze, all of which were found in front of the portico of the southeast facade of the Porticus Deorum Consentium and on the podium of the Temple of Vespasian. Instead of coming from these buildings themselves, it is likely that these fragments were found at the base of the supporting wall by Napoleon's excavators who dug in Rome during the French occupation

between 1811 and 1813.[12] It is not clear whether there were any further stories, but no elements in a third order have ever been found. Various reconstructions give the building a facade much like the frons scaenae of a theater in front of a solid block-like third storey (Fig. 3),[13] or a stoa-like facade in front of an open atrium (Fig. 4 and Fig. 5 and Fig. 6).[14]

Clearly the building served as much as a connector between the two promontories of the Capitoline hill as it did as a building set at and above the northern end of the Roman Forum. A stairway from the Forum up through the building to the Capitoline is one of two axes which dominate the orientation and the form of the building, just as in Michelangelo's later Palazzo Senatorio which was built on top of its remains.[15] One could easily say that the main axes, in fact, were those of the walkways which ran east-west across the facade of the structure and which gave access to rooms along both the upper portico and the lower arcade.

The identification and date of this building are given by two inscriptions. One was included in an early corpus

[9] This paper was written initially in 1994. Since then Diane Favro's book, The Urban Image of Augustan Rome, 1996, has appeared. In this innovative survey the author focuses attention on the changes made to the topography of Rome during the period between 52 B.C. and A.D. 14 which she brackets laudably with before-and-after descriptions of walks through important districts of the city by two fictional observers. The author's goal is to ascribe the major transformation of Rome's urban image, in terms both of specific buildings and in the way the city was viewed, to the princeps Augustus and others associated with him. Whereas Favro seems to take the concept of cityscape as a given notion and considers the Republican city to have had little unity beyond the presence of separate building ensembles (cf. p.167–180), it is the argument of the present paper that the Capitoline hill as seen from the Forum did have a coherent skyline profile by the time of the Late Republic and that the concept of cityscape itself was a product of this development.

[10] General topographic descriptions of this area appear in G. Lugli, Itinerario di Roma Antica, 1970, p. 133–139 (with actual state pictures), and Samuel Ball Platner and Thomas Ashby, A Topographical Dictionary of Ancient Rome, 1929, p. 506–508. See now Lawrence Richardson Jr., A New Topographical Dictionary of Ancient Rome, 1992, p. 376–377 and Lexicon Topographicum Urbis Romae, Vol. Primo A–C, E.M. Steinby, ed. 1993, p. 226–234. Regarding the building's later history including its transformation into the Palazzo Senatorio, see G. C. Argan and B. Contardi, Michelangelo architetto, 1990, p. 252–263, Mario Maieri Elia, La Loggia Squarcialupi in Campidoglio (e un'ipotesi sulla Scala Senatoria), Architettura, Storia e Documenti 1986/2, p. 79–86, and H. Thies, Michelangelo Das Kapitol, Italienische Forschungen, Dritte Folge, Band 11, 1982, pp. 14–16 with figs 3–5, who recognizes the importance of this structure as a connective element between the Capitoline hill and the Arx, p.16: "Und da die Kammlinie des Doppelhuegels einen gegen di Stadt geoeffneten Bogen bildet, scheinen die Architekturen, parallel oder orthogonal dazu angeordnet, wie gefaechert auf einen gemeinsamen Brennpunkt im Stadtkoerper selbst bezogen zu sein."

[11] R. Delbrueck, Hellenistische Bauten in Latium, I, 1907, J.H. Parker, Archaeology of Rome 5, Forum Romanum et Magnum, 1879, p. 23–46, plates III–IX. A detailed series of actual state plans and elevations also appear in J.H. Parker, The Archaeology of Rome, The Primitive Fortifications of the City of Rome, 1878, plates I–VIII and XI–XII.

[12] Delbrueck, op. cit., p.44. For detailed discussion of the Napoleonic excavations in and around the so-called Tabularium, see Ronald T. Ridley, The Eagle and the Spade, Archaeology in Rome during the Napoleonic era, 1992, p. 180–182.

[13] See the reconstruction by Delbrueck, cit in note 11., plate III, and the model at the University of Paris (Sorbonne) of the 1930s which clearly is based upon it in P. Bigot, Rome Antique au IV^e Siecle Ap. J.C., 1955.

[14] See the watercolour reconstruction of 1866 by Constant Moyaux which appears in M. Ragon, "Roma antiqua", Connaissance des Arts 412, 1986, p. 100–105, here, fig. p. 101. A similar reconstruction is given to the so-called Tabularium in the well-known model now in the Museum of Roman Civilization (EUR district) at Rome shown in A guide to the Monumental Centre of Ancient Rome, with Reconstructions of the Monuments, Roma, 1966: opposite p.22; see also the reconstruction in M.F. Hoffbauer and H. Thedenat, Le Forum Romain et la voie sacrée, 1905, p. 83. A rare reconstruction showing the northern side of the building by J. Buehlmann and A. von Wagner appears in F.R. Cowell, Everyday Life in Ancient Rome, 1961, figure 3 opposite p.19.

[15] This stairway appears in many publications; cf. G. Lugli, Itinerario di Roma Antica, Milan, 1970, p. 135, fig. 81 and B. Brizzi, Roma: i monumenti antichi, Rome, 1973, p. 38. For design considerations in the building by Michelangelo, see Thies, cit. in note 10, p. 14–16.

of inscriptions by Nicolò Signorili[16] and already lost before the end of the XV Century. It read (CIL VI 1314):

Q LVTATIVS Q F Q [n] CATVLVS COS / SVB-STRVCTIONEM ET TABVLARIVM / DE S S FACIVNDVM COERAVIT [ei]DEMQVE / PRO[bavit].[17]

This inscription seems to have been found, corroded by salt, in a storage room at the northern end of the facade. The other inscription was found in 1845 close to where it is today on a block of tufa in a doorway leading into a room facing the Roman Forum below on the southeast end. It reads (CIL VI 1313):

q lu]TATIVS Q F Q N C[atulus cos / de s]EN SENT FACIVNDV[m coeravit] EIDEMQVE PROB[avit][18]

We know that Quintus Lutatius Catulus was consul in 78 B.C., and a funerary inscription re-used in the Fatebene-fratelli Hospital on the Tiber island seems to give us the name of an architect who may have actually planned and executed the building:

L CORNELIVS L F VOT / Q CATVLI COS PRAEF FABR / CENSORIS ARCHITECTVS[19]

It is not known whether these inscriptions were contemporary with the original building – Delbrueck seemed to think that the style of the preserved Doric columns was Flavian and that the inscription might be the same kind of retrojection that we see in the famous inscription on the Pantheon, a building constructed in the time of Hadrian, which modestly refers to its original predecessor built by Marcus Vipsanius Agrippa.[20] Others have suggested that

the structure originally dates prior to the time of Quintus Lutatius Catulus and that Catulus was simply charged with the restoration of a previously existing Tabularium,[21] but the presence of a Republican structure burned in the fire of 83 B.C. beneath one of the rooms of the so-called Tabularium offers a terminus post quem for construction of that building.[22]

It has long been commented that the origin of this building type and of its placement may be found in the architecture of the Hellenistic east. Whereas buildings and cities of Classical type imposed a form on the landscape, sometimes to almost absurd extremes such as the grid-planned city of Priene set on a mountain slope, later Hellenistic architectural design sought to adapt the buildings to the given landscape, such as the city of Pergamon which follows the contour of the mountain upon which it is set.[23] This kind of architectural coordination with the landscape may be seen not only in the layout of entire cities but also in that of particular sanctuary-complexes.[24] In the Sanctuary of Asklepios on the island of Kos which dates to the late Third or early Second century B.C. the observer's view is defined by wide, open courts, and is directed by colonnades which define the edges of the courts toward a spectacular panorama.[25] A more subtle visual process occurs as one approaches from afar, particularly in the Second century B.C. Sanctuary of Athena Lindaia on the island of Rhodes. Vincent Scully has called this process an act of loss and rediscovery as one first approaches the sanctuary.[26] The sanctuary and the promontory act

---

[16] N. Signorili, Descriptio Urbis Romae, before 1431 quoted in A. Van Heck, Breviarium Urbis Romae Antiquae, 1977, n.137.3.

[17] CIL VI 1314: "The consul Quintus Lutatius Catulus, son of Quintus [and] grandson of Quintus, by degree of the Senate had the foundation (substructionem) and the records office (Tabularium) made and he certified it."

[18] CIL VI 1313: "The consul Quintus Lutatius Catulus, son of Quintus [and] grandson of Quintus, by decree of the Senate had it made and he approved it."

[19] Giulio Molisani, "Lucius Cornelius Quinti Catuli Architectus," Rendiconti dei Lincei, 8, 26, p. 41–49 with the inscription on p. 42: "Lucius Cornelius Voturia son of Lucius, prefect of the builders in the consulate of Quintus Lutatius Catulus and architect while he (Quintus Lutatius Catulus) was censor."

[20] Delbrueck, cit. in note 11, p. 46.

[21] Molisani, cit. in note 19, p. 44 (citing Lugli). It is known that the building was restored under the emperor Claudius in A.D. 46; cf. Lawrence Richardson Jr., A New Topographical Dictionary of Ancient Rome, 1992, p. 376.

[22] A. M. Sommella, "L'esplorazione archeologica per il restauro del Tabularium," Archeologia Laziale 6, 1984, p. 159–163: 160 and n.5.

[23] Margaret Lyttelton, Baroque Architecture in Classical Antiquity, 1974, p. 208–210.

[24] Lyttelton, cit. in note 23, p. 207–208. See general discussion of the setting for Hellenistic sanctuaries in Spiro Kostof, A History of Architecture, Settings and Rituals, 1995, p. 170–174.

[25] Architectural control of the viewer's field of vision in this manner is included among the characteristics defined by M. Lyttelton as 'ancient baroque' (Lyttelton, cit. in note 23, ch. 1, esp. pp. 13–14).

together as a whole giving recognizable form to the summit on which it is placed. As one gets closer, the sanctuary actually disappears from sight as one's field of vision is taken up more by the mass of the promontory itself. Only when one ascends the promontory and arrives in the open court areas do the architectural features which were visible from afar come back into view – and dramatically closer! Once inside the sanctuary, one's vision is widened to the spectacular panorama which may be seen looking outwards from the sanctuary's colonnaded courts. Further penetration of the sanctuary's interior brings the viewer to the actual temple in the final act of re-discovery.

Two sanctuaries in Italy demonstrate the same characteristics as the sanctuaries on Kos and Rhodes – the Temple of Jupiter Anxur at Terracina, and the Sanctuary of Fortuna Primigenia at modern Palestrina. Although we do not know the names of the architects who designed them nor the builders who constructed them, the close similarities and the date in the mid-Second Century B.C.E. together make it likely that they were inspired directly by the Hellenistic sanctuaries of the Aegean.

The Temple of Jupiter Anxur is set on top of a promontory overlooking the Tyrrhenian Sea.[27] Like its Aegean counterparts, it is a recognizable detail on the summit of the promontory and one must rediscover it by first losing sight of it in the ascent to the top. A platform set on archways running on the north, west, and south creates a court for a temple which is almost hidden, ironically, by the open space. The archways themselves, built in opus incertum with cut-stone block quoining, play with the viewer's sense of depth. While this sanctuary is a distinct architectural complex, it could not have been built or moved anywhere else because its position on the promontory necessitated some of its fundamental elements, such as the platform, and therefore it is, indeed, part of the landscape.

Similarly, the Sanctuary of Fortuna Primigenia rests bound uniquely to the hillside on which it is constructed giving an experience of re-discovery to the hardy soul who wishes to climb all the way up.[28] Two covered passageways lead from north and south up to a central staircase which follows the axis across which the sanctuary has been designed symmetrically. Ascending the stairway one passes two platform-courts very similar in form to the platform courts on Kos and Rhodes. Finally, one arrives at the last stairway which leads to the center of a theatral area dominated by an imposing semi-circular facade. Originally, the facade had a colonnade; today, the Sixteenth Century Palazzo Barberini maintains the shape if not the precise appearance.

The features common to these Italian sanctuaries and the so-called Tabularium at Rome are obvious, and no one denies that they belong to the same architectural tradition. The structure itself is supported by heavy walls, and its architecture includes a colonnade and an arcade built in cement and stone. So too, the so-called Tabularium could not have stood anywhere other than the place in which it was constructed. Long covered stairways take a person up through the face of the building. Although there seem to have been no open courts along the facade, the observer's panorama is directed out toward the Roman Forum (and we do not really know how much more of a structure there was above the preserved lower arcade). Furthermore, the date of the so-called Tabularium does not seem to be too much later than those of the Italic temples.

So what is different about the complex at Rome? I believe that the difference lies in the architectural context in which it was built – whereas both the Aegean and the Italian sanctuaries tied buildings to the natural forms of the land around them, the so-called Tabularium is linked also to the buildings already in existence around it, thereby creating a sort of artificial landscape, or cityscape. To the east and west of the so-called Tabularium lay important temples which had stood individually against the sky in one form or another for centuries – the first Temple of Jupiter Optimus Maximus was completed before the end of the Sixth Century B.C. and rebuilt following a devastating fire in 83 B.C. by the same consul Quintus Lutatius Catulus and his architect Lucius Cornelius who built the so-called Tabularium;[29] the Temple of Juno Moneta (which has yet to be found) may have been built in 345 B.C., in

---

[26] Vincent Scully, The Earth, the Temple and the Gods, Greek Sacred Architecture, 1979, p. 199–201.

[27] F. Coarelli, I Santuari del Lazio in età Repubblicana, Studi Nuova Italia Scientifica, Archeologia 7, 1987, ch. 5, p. 113–140; H. Kaehler, Das Fortunaheiligtum von Palestrina Praeneste, in F. Coarelli ed., Studi su Praeneste, 1978, p. 221–272.

---

[28] Here we should note how the Italian platform rests on arches built in *opus incertum* in contrast to the ashlar masonry used in the Greek East.

any case probably before the so-called Tabularium.[30] In front of the imposing foundation structure of the so-called Tabularium were the Temple of Concord, symbol of the agreement between plebeians and patricians in 367 B.C. but which was actually built only in 121 B.C., and the Porticus Deorum Consentium, which had since 174 B.C. been the fundamental dramatic backdrop of the northern end of the Roman Forum.[31]

Paul Zanker, in his widely discussed Power of Images in the Age of Augustus, considers the creation of the so-called Tabularium to be an expression of the dominance of the Optimates in the Senate who had supported the dictatorship of Lucius Cornelius Sulla.[32] We should not underestimate Sulla's architectural agenda nor the significance of the so-called Tabularium.[33] The panorama which one sees when standing in the Roman Forum looking up toward the Capitoline is dominated not so much by the Temple of Concord as by the so-called Tabularium which links the buildings to the sky (Fig. 7). In a similar manner, the view out from the Tabularium over the Roman Forum is a bird's-eye view which adds a third dimension of depth to the kind of profile view one sees in a skyline (Fig. 8). But these effects are more subtle than a simple equation of political iconography, and I believe that they reflect a more fundamental process behind the urbanization of Rome and its image as the Eternal City – the formation of the cityscape itself as an urban reality and as a concept which almost naturally had repercussions on Roman art.

Prior to the Second century B.C. one does not find profile views of cities – only the barest representation of a battlement can be seen in the upper register of the famous painting from a tomb dating to the Third Century B.C. on the Esquiline hill, which shows a Roman and a Samnite general making peace.[34] But landscape was not an unknown element in the art of early Italy. Ross Holloway has underscored the importance of the sky itself as a feature in Etruscan tomb paintings as early as the Sixth century B.C. In the famous Tomb of Hunting and Fishing at Tarquinia, fishermen in a boat on the sea gather their nets beneath a wide expanse of the sky filled with birds. A hunter tries to hit one of the birds using a slingshot. Rocks and the sea border the scene, but it is the sky that is the most important feature of the scene.[35]

Roman interest in the sky can be traced back to Etruscan religion and the practice of augury – that is, reading signs from the gods in the flight of birds. Romulus and Remus supposedly practiced augury in founding their respective settlements on the Palatine and the Aventine hills in the Roman's foundation-myth.[36] The northeastern promontory of the Capitoline hill, the Arx, was the site of Rome's auguraculum – the spot where the city's augurs read the flight of birds for each new month.[37] The location for the Capitolium at Rome was chosen specifically on a height which would dominate the area around it and at the same time stand out against the sky. Roman colonies such as Cosa have a temple placed on a height in the mid-Second century B.C.;[38] at Pompeii the Civic Forum is dominated by a Capitolium. But a temple set against the sky is not the same as a multiple-building skyline, which can only be seen at Rome towards the end of the Republic.

We are hampered in our efforts to understand the visual representations of Rome because of the lack of material from the earlier centuries of the Republic; nevertheless, we do not seem to see buildings on coinage or in other forms of art until the famous buildings of the Late Republic such as the Temple of Jupiter Optimus

[29] Richardson, cit. in note 21, p. 221–224. The fire of 83 B.C. is mentioned by many ancient authors.

[30] Ibidem, p. 215.

[31] Of course, the Temple of Vespasian was a later addition; ibidem, p. 412.

[32] Paul Zanker, The Power of Images in the Age of Augustus, trans. A. Shapiro, 1988, p. 21.

[33] Favro, cit. in note 9, p. 56 rightly notes that no source directly connects the dictator Lucius Cornelius Sulla with this building but its inclusion in a Sullan building program would seem to be all but inevitable.

[34] Ranuccio Bianchi Bandinelli, Rome the Center of Power, 500 B.C. to A.D. 200, 1970, p. 113 (illustration), and p. 115–116 (discussion).

[35] R. Ross Holloway, Conventions of Etruscan Painting in the Tomb of Hunting and Fishing at Tarquinii, American Journal of Archaeology 69, 1965, p. 341–347, here p. 342. The sky in this painting recalls the 'sheltering sky' in the film The Sheltering Sky directed by Bernardo Bertolucci (Warner Brothers Pictures, produced by Jeremy Thomas, 1991).

[36] Livy, I, vi.3–vii.2 (on the contest of augury between Romulus and Remus for the foundation of Rome).

[37] Richardson, cit. in note 21, p. 45; S.V. 'auguraculum (1)'.

[38] On the arx, or citadel, of Cosa, see Frank E. Brown, Cosa the Making of a Roman Town, 1980, ch. IV, pp. 47–62.

Maximus and the Basilica Aemilia.[39] Later buildings are shown on coins with increasing sophistication – not only is a profile view given, but also a bird's-eye view of the interior adding that third dimension of depth.[40] Finally, we see the fully evolved image of the city as a building cluster in imperial issues (Fig. 9).[41]

Building-clusters appear in other media already in the Late Republic. Perhaps the best-known such representation appears in the polychrome mosaic found, in fact, within the same Sanctuary of Fortuna Primigenia at Palestrina and ascribed by Pliny the Elder (N.H., XXXVI, 189) to the time of Lucius Cornelius Sulla.[42] This same bird's-eye perspective appears in a wall-painting from the House of the Priest Amandius at Pompeii which shows Daedalus flying and the ill-fated Icarus falling over a walled city which is interpreted as the city of Knossos (Fig. 10).[43] The city comprises not only the wall which surrounds and defines it but also the series of characteristic buildings which make up its interior.

Why was there such a sudden interest in landscapes and cityscapes in the Late Republic? Peter Holliday has argued that panels bearing perspective paintings and identifying placards were an important part of Roman triumphal processions.[44] He argues that Andrea Mantegna's painting The Triumphs of Caesar (c.1474–78), a reconstruction of the triumph of 46 B.C. following Julius Caesar's defeat of the Gauls (which unfortunately has not been preserved for us in any detail in our Classical literary sources), nevertheless may well capture the essence of the images carried in procession.[45] In Mantegna's painting we see placards bearing both verbal messages and images of cityscapes borne along at intervals throughout the procession. Holliday, whose focus was upon reception theory in art, argued that the placards were necessary in order for the spectator to complete the meaning of the scenes – the placards helped the observer package and label in his mind

---

[39] Denarii of M. Volteius (78 or 74 B.C.) and Petillius Capitolinus (c.41 B.C.) commemorate the reconstruction and restoration, respectively of the temple of Jupiter Optimus Maximus (the one created by Quintus Lutatius Catulus) and its cult-statue (P.V. Hill, The Monuments of Ancient Rome as Coin Types, 1989, p. 24–25), while a coin minted in 61 B.C. by M. Aemilius Lepidus commemorates the Basilica Aemilia which had been restored in 80–78 B.C. (ibidem, p. 41–42 with fig. 61). B. Brizzi, Roma: i monumenti antichi, Roma, 1973, pp. 297–300 also presents a series of Republican and early Imperial monuments shown on coins. It is surprising that we have yet to find a coin representing the so-called Tabularium!

[40] A sestertius of Titus, dated to A.D. 80/81 shows the Colosseum, the Meta Sudans, and a portion of Nero's Golden House (Hill, cit. in note 39, p. 40 and 41, fig. 60).

[41] A sestertius of Trajan minted in A.D. 103 on the occasion of the emperor's restoration of the Circus Maximus shows the complex of structures which made up the Circus from the Forum Boarium with the Duodecim Portae (12 entrances), a gateway arch and two other arches, a hexastyle shrine of Sol, the metae (goals) at each end of the spina (raceway median), a central obelisk, an equestrian statue of Trajan and a shrine of Cybele with deliberate distortion (the spina is set across the raceway at right angles to its correct orientation) in order to represent prominently the monuments which Trajan had restored (Hill, op. cit., p. 46–47 with figure 72, also F. Castagnoli, et al., Topografia e Urbanistica di Roma, 1958, tav. XXXIV, 1).

Discussion of perspective in city representation on later imperial coins appears in Martin Jessup Price and Bluma L. Trell, Coins and their Cities, Architecture on the ancient coins of Greece, Rome and Palestine, 1977, p. 24–33. A coin minted for Philippus Senior, 244–249 A.C., at Bizya in Thrace shows a city-wall, a gate (perhaps a porta triumphalis), a forum and temple, and perhaps (Baldwin Smith) royal baths (see ibid., p. 25, fig. 24). A similar composition showing buildings enclosed within a fortification wall appears on a coin of Gordian III (238–244 A.C.) from Marcianopolis in Thrace (see Price and Trell, cit., p. 25, fig. 25).

[42] For discussion of the representation of buildings in this mosaic see P.G.P. Meyboom, The Nile Mosaic of Palestrina, Early Evidence of Egyptian Religion in Italy, 1995, p. 184 and p. 368–369, n. 11. In this mosaic the focus seems to be on the river and on the appearance of Romans in Egypt which for them was a land of wonders; we do see clusters of structures in a sort of bird's-eye perspective which likens them to natural land-forms. While perspective painting using receding lines was a technique present in Greek painting in the Fifth century B.C., the earliest representation of a town using a 'bird's-eye' vantage point would seem to date no earlier than the Third century B.C. (ibidem, p. 184).

[43] H.P. Von Blanckenhagen, Daedalus and Icarus on Pompeian Walls, Mitteilungen des Deutsches Archaeologisches Instituts, Roemische Abteilung 75, 1968, p. 106–143.

[44] P. Holliday, Roman Triumphal Painting: Its Function, Development, and Reception, The Art Bulletin, 79, 1997, p. 130–147.

[45] Andrew Martindale notes how in Mantegna's painting a recurrent code of building-types which recalled the massive stature, the loftiness and the geometrical forms of classical architecture (Andrew Martindale, The Triumphs of Caesar by Andrea Mantegna in the Collection of Her Majesty the Queen at Hampton Court, 1979, p. 132): "... formed part of the current 'shorthand' to indicate either 'Rome' or, less frequently, the 'classical past'…"

the messages of place and conquest which literally paraded in front of him.

Some literary and visual evidence for the use of city images in triumphs has been preserved. The Republican orator and statesman Cicero (In Pisonem, 60) mentions 'models of [captured] towns' (simulacra oppidorum) which were paraded in a Roman triumph, as does the historian Livy (XXXVII.59.3) in connection with the triumph of Scipio Asiaticus in 188 B.C.[46] Placards appear in the relief along the interior of the Arch of Titus showing the spoils from the sack of Jerusalem.[47] Clearly the notion of an urban center was expressed both in terms of words and images in the context of a triumph, and it is reasonable to suppose that in order to express the identity of a specific captured city it was necessary to represent certain readily identifiable buildings or perhaps buildings clustered into a true cityscape.

Other painting and relief sculpture illustrate both how common constructed cityscapes became during the Roman Empire and the way in which the complex interaction of single buildings and the city profile was recognized and employed by Roman artists to represent urban environments.[48] The seaside villas presented in wall-paintings from Gragnano and other locations around the Bay of Naples are in effect miniature cities – architectural complexes which themselves become landscapes.[49] The copy of the famous relief from Avezzano formerly in the Museo Torlonia at Rome shows both the wall of a town and its conglomeration of buildings on the inside and other features outside the wall.[50] Arguably the most famous cityscape from Roman antiquity was painted on the wall of a bedroom in the villa of Publius Fannius Sinistor at Boscoreale now in the Metropolitan Museum of Art in New York City. Here a somewhat erratic, incoherent combination of perspective-lines gives nonetheless a pleasing view of urban buildings which may have been derived from back-

drop paintings created for the Roman stage.[51] Another famous cityscape shows the amphitheater of Pompeii and the buildings immediately around it during the brawl of A.D. 59 described by the historian Tacitus (Annales, XIV,

---

[48] The recent fortuitous discovery of a fresco at Rome beneath the Baths of Trajan on the wall of a passageway which may have been part of Nero's Golden House provides new perspective on the Roman's notion of cityscape during the imperial period (see discussion by B. van der Meer and J.-T. Bakker and preliminary images available on the internet at the ROMARCH web-site and related web-links). The scale of the fresco (it covers a surface area at least 3.6 by 2.75 meters) is comparable only to the fragmentary Marble Plan of Rome produced during the reign of Septimius Severus and placed in Vespasian's Temple of Peace. Proposals for the precise city represented range from Rome itself, to Ostia, Naples, and other locations outside of Italy, and the proposed dates range from Nero's reign (both before and after the fire of A.D. 64), to the reigns of Trajan and Hadrian, to even the Third century A.C. Nicholas Purcell, A panorama of ancient Rome, Nature, 392, April 9, 1998, p. 545–547, notes the generous amount of open space which is shown within the city's walls, as well as the dense packing of private dwellings which are dominated by large public monuments, and he relates it to Rome indirectly. Whatever the subject and the date may be, it is clear that the composition is made up of major, ostensibly recognizable monuments set within a wall which defines the immediate limits of the city and that the city as a whole is the subject of the painting rather than an ancillary background element to some other subject. The full and proper publication of this fresco should be awaited eagerly.

[49] See Bettina Ann Bergmann, Varia topia: architectural landscapes in Roman painting of the late Republic and early empire, dissertation, Columbia University, 1986, who considers architecture in Campanian paintings to be restricted ultimately to individual buildings, but who (p. 370) recognizes the city-like qualities of buildings set around a lake in Nero's Golden House as described by Tacitus (Annales, XV.40–43) and Suetonius (Nero, 31).

[50] Links, cit. in note 2, p. 5, dates this relief to the First century A.C., while William A. MacDonald, The Architecture of the Roman Empire, Volume II, 1986, p. 50, ill. 45 ascribes it to the Second century A.C.

[51] For a general description of the villa and its paintings see M. Anderson, Pompeian Frescoes in the Metropolitan Museum of Art, The Metropolitan Museum of Art Bulletin, Winter, 1987/88, p. 17–36. An image of the cityscape itself appears in R. Ross Holloway, "Il cubicolo della villa romana di Boscoreale nel Metropolitan Museum of Art, New York," in Rendiconti della Pontificia Accademia Romana di Archeologia, 62, 1989–1990, p. 105–119. On the relation of this painting to the Roman stage, see Richard Beacham, The Roman Theatre and Its Audience, 1991, pp. 177–17 and fig. 24.

---

[46] Sources cited by Favro, cit. in note 9, p. 53. Livy, Ab Urbe Condita, XXXVII.59.3: "[Scipio Asiaticus] Tulit in triumpho signa militaria ducenta viginti quattuor, oppidorum simulacra centum triginta quattuor, …/[Scipio Asiaticus] bore in triumph two hundred twenty-four military standards, one hundred thirty-four models of [captured] towns …" These descriptions would seem to be the source for the description of a typical Roman triumph in Zonaras, Epitome, VII.21.

[47] Richardson, cit. in note 21, p. 30, cf. Arcus Titi (2), M. Pfanner, Der Titusbogen, 1983.

17), and it employs the same combination of profile and bird's-eye views one finds in Roman coinage in order to provide the greatest amount of visual information.[52] Scenes shown on Trajan's column represent recognizable building-types if not specific buildings.[53] The sculptural frieze added to the Arch of Constantine shows the actual buildings of the Roman forum.[54]

Early Christian mosaics also incorporate cityscape and sometimes even a true skyline. The mosaic in the rear apse of the Church of Santa Pudenziana at Rome dated to A.D. 390 shows a cityscape as a background to the Pantokrator.[55] At Ravenna, in the Church of S. Apollinare Nuovo (late Fifth Century A.C. – ca. 490) a similar array of buildings is set against the gold background.[56]

Two mosaic views of Jerusalem illustrate the representational methods – in a mosaic on the triumphal arch of the Church of Santa Maria Maggiore at Rome (ca. A.D. 435), Jerusalem is shown in bird's-eye perspective and labeled.[57] In the well-known mosaic map of Madaba in Jordan which is dated to the mid-Sixth century A.C., Jerusalem is shown as the elliptical outline of the city wall with specific, recognizable buildings arranged somewhat symmetrically across a central street.[58] These two mosaics show how the way in which an artist renders a city is really a matter of struggle or compromise between two techniques of representation – 1) the natural rendering of the buildings and the landscape in horizontal profile, and 2) the planimetric mapping of topographic features arranged according to an abstract geometric formula. While such a compromise may seem to us to be simply an intellectual exercise,[59] the development of the cityscape in the Roman world would seem to have emerged out of the direct, empirical observation of the skyline of Rome, once it had been built.[60]

When we think about the symbolization of the city through perspective painting and representations of it, we should think about our own experience. An interesting study was performed in Rome and Milan in the 1970s by Donata Francescato and William Mebane.[61] They asked 118 people (selected according to parameters of class, age, sex and residence) to create image maps of Rome and Milan through their responses to a series of questions. They discovered that modern Romans were particularly drawn to locational reference points – to monuments, particularly those of its historical district (i.e. roughly the area within the Aurelian walls). People over thirty were more likely to remember particular monuments than those under thirty who especially recalled pathways presumably because learning one's way around the city is a new and exciting thing.[62] Middle-class interviewees tended to identify more elements than lower-class individuals whose view of the city seemed to revolve around the home. In the

---

[52] Cf. Holliday, cit.in note 44, p. 140, fig. 7.

[53] F. Lepper and S. Frere, Trajan's Column, A New Edition of the Cichorius Plates, 1988, S. Settis, La Colonna Traiana, 1988.

[54] B. Berenson, The Arch of Constantine; or The decline of form, 1954; Richardson cit. in note 21, p. 24–25, S.V. 'Arcus Constantini'. In this relief Constantine and retinue are seated on Rostra, column of Tetrarch's monument, to the left the Basilica Julia and the Arch of Tiberius, to the right the Arch of Septimius Severus.

[55] G. Matthiae, Mosaici Medioevali delle Chiese di Roma, 1967, p. 55–76 and figs. 36, 46–47; J. Wilpert and W. N. Schumacher, Die Roemischen Mosaiken der Kirchlichen Bauten vom IV.–XIII. Jahrhundert, 1976, p. 306–307 with plates 20–22.

[56] A. Lorizzo, The Mosaics of Ravenna, 1976, p. 29–34 with figs. 11–12.

[57] Wilpert and Schumacher, cit.in note 55, p. 318 with plate 72.

[58] H. Donner, The Mosaic Map of Madaba, An Introductory Guide, 1992, esp. p. 87–94 (analytical description of the mosaic); M. Piccirillo, The Mosaics of Jordan, The American Center of Oriental Research Publication No. 1, 1993, pp. 81–95; Meir Ben Dov and Yoel Rappel, Mosaics of the Holy Land, 1987, p. 114–117.

[59] See Boudewijn Bakker, Kaarten, boeken en prenten. De topografische traditie in de Noordelijke Nederlanden/Maps, Books and Prints. The Topographical Tradition in the Northern Netherlands in Opkomst en bloei van het Noordnederlandse stadsgezicht in de 17de eeuw/The Dutch Cityscape in the 17th Century and Its Sources, Amsterdams Historisch Museum 17 juni t/m 28 augustus 1977, Art Gallery of Ontario, Toronto, September 27 to November 13, 1977, 1977, p. 66–75.

[60] The development of Euclid's theory of optics in the Third century B.C. may have had a similar, practical inspiration from the proliferation in the Hellenistic era of the Greek stoa. See John Onians, Art and Thought in the Hellenistic Age, The Greek World View 350–50 B.C., 1979, p. 175–178 with particular emphasis on the sanctuaries on Kos and Rhodes which we have discussed.

[61] Donata Francescato and William Mebane, How Citizens View Two Great Cities: Milan and Rome, in R. Downs and D. Stea, eds., Image and Environment, Cognitive Mapping and Spatial Behavior, 1973, ch. 8, p. 131–147.

case of Milan, native residents seemed to have a much more complete mental image of the city than non-natives.

It would be interesting to do something of this sort with the inhabitants of ancient Rome in order to measure the impact of skyline architecture on their own perceptions of the city, but unfortunately that is not possible. What we can do is glean from two literary passages from Late Antiquity the sense of grandeur which architecture had given to the city over the centuries and the way in which it seemed to bolster Rome's image as the Eternal City both as a physical reality and as a notion even when Rome as a power was crumbling. We read in De reditu suo [I, 47–60] a panegyric written by Claudius Rutilius Namatianus in 416 A.C., six years after city had been sacked by Visigoths:[63]

> Hear, O queen most beautiful of your own world, Rome, received amid the starry vaults! Hear, mother of men and mother of gods, through your temples we are not far from heaven: you we chant, and as long as the fates permit, shall forever chant. No one, while living can be unmindful of you … You have made a single fatherland [patriam] out of diverse peoples; your dominion has been a benefit to those who had no law. And by offering to the conquered incorporation into your law you have made a city where formerly there was a world [Urbem fecisti, quod prius orbis erat].

Here the verbal image of the city (urbs) is used to symbolize the notion of a unified and orderly society under the Roman empire which Namatianus valued. One hundred and thirty-one years later, a letter said to have been written by the Byzantine general Belisarius to Totila in A.D. 547 and included in the text of Procopius of Caesarea captures the meaning which the sum-total of Rome's monuments still must have given to the city. Totila had captured Rome and was considering whether or not to raze the

city's monuments in response to a military defeat in Lucania (VII, xxii, 9–12)[64]:

> Now among all the cities under the sun Rome is agreed to be the greatest and the most noteworthy. For it has not been created by the ability of one man, nor has it attained such greatness and beauty by a power of short duration, but a multitude of monarchs, many companies of the best men, a great lapse of time, and an extraordinary abundance of wealth have availed to bring together in that city all other things that are in the whole world, and skilled workers besides. Thus, little by little, have they built the city, such as you behold it, thereby leaving to future generations memorials of the ability of them all, so that insult to these monuments would properly be considered a great crime against the men of all time; for by such action the men of former generations are robbed of the memorials of their ability, and future generations of the sight of their works.

Totila wisely chose not to go ahead with his plan.

While neither of these passages speaks directly of a visual cityscape it is clear that Rome was considered to be the sum of the accomplishments of many individuals over many generations and that what made Rome *Rome* came to be appreciated in retrospect. By analogy, the cohesion of Rome's buildings into an architectural landscape, a process begun already under the Republic by the time of the creation of the so-called Tabularium and carried forward through the course of the First century A.C. and the 'High Empire' of the Second century, served to formulate a visual image of the city which was more than that of any single building or monument. The lasting effect of both the image and the physical reality of ancient Rome can be seen in the architecture above the Roman Forum which survives to this day – while we may laud Michelangelo's Palazzo Senatorio, we must admit that his design was constrained greatly by the presence of the venerable Roman structure on which it stood and that his work was to some degree a matter of renewal, not replacement. The ancient reality in Rome's current cityscape reminds us of the city's history and identity, and it encourages us to recognize and respect the inherent meaning of place in the cities we build today.

---

[62] The importance of pathways recalls William MacDonald's concept of the 'urban armature' in Roman city planning (see MacDonald, cit. in note 50, 1986: chapter 2, pp. 5–31). In effect, the armature presents the city as a series of connected experiences – temples and other public structures are set alongside major streets which are the focus of and which thrust the observer's gaze along corridors which are punctuated by gateways and other forms of connective architecture.

[63] Latin text found in Rutilio Namaziano, Il Ritorno, a cura di Alessandro Fo, 1992, p. 6.

[64] Trans. H.B. Dewing from Procopius, 4, Loeb Classical Library, p. 347. The author wishes to thank Dr. Charles Pazdernik for bringing this passage to his attention.

**Fig. 1.** Postcard view of Seattle with buildings outlined. Photo David S. Curran, permission Smith-Western Co.

**Fig. 2.** Three words with outlines.

**Fig. 3.** Facade reconstuction from Delbrueck.

**Fig. 4.** Watercolour reconstruction (1866) by Constant Moyaux after Ragon. Note the Doric arcade along the upper storey.

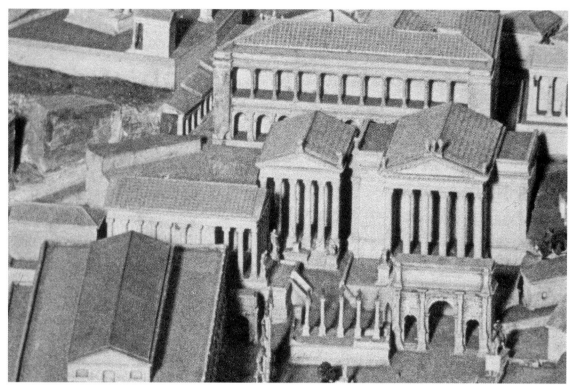

**Fig. 5.** Detail of model in Museum of Roman Civilization, EUR, Rome. The so-called Tabularium appears above the Forum in the upper portion of the frame.

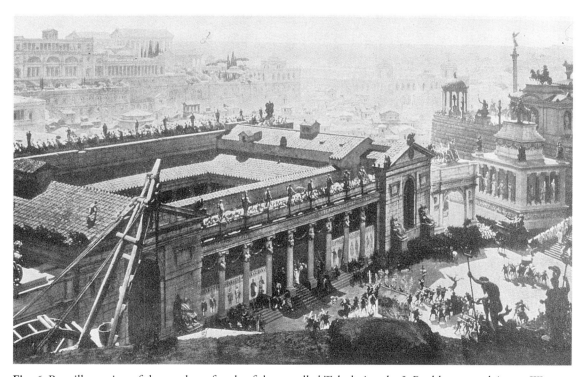

**Fig. 6.** Rare illustration of the northern facade of the so-called Tabularium by J. Buehlmann and A. von Wagner after Cowell.

**Fig. 7.** Watercolour reconstruction of the Roman Forum towards the Capitoline after Hoffbauer and Thedenat.

**Fig. 8.** Watercolour reconstruction of the Capitoline towards the Roman Forum after Hoffbauer and Thedenat.

**Fig. 9.** Coin of Philippus Senior, 244–249 A.C. issued at Bizya from Price and Trell.

**Fig. 10.** Fresco illustrating the Flight of Daedalus and Icarus from the House of the Priest Amandius at Pompeii, after Von Blanckenhagen.

# FAMILY VALUES: ANCESTRAL REPRESENTATION AND SOCIAL REPRODUCTION IN ROMAN HOUSES

*Owen Doonan*

A preliminary version of this paper was presented at the 1995 NEH Summer Seminar for College Teachers held at the American Academy in Rome entitled "Death, Commemoration and Society in Ancient Rome". I would like to thank the seminar leaders R. Saller and J. Bodel and participants (especially E. D'Ambra) for their suggestions. R. Saller read a draft of the manuscript and allowed me to read and cite several forthcoming articles. C. King kindly allowed me to read several chapters from his dissertation (Univ. of Chicago 1998) and made many valuable suggestions on an early draft of this paper. Finally, thanks are extended to the Department of Classical Languages and Literatures of the University of Chicago for hosting me as a Visiting Scholar during the academic years 1995–99. Finally, I would like to thank R. Ross Holloway for urging me to study pre-Roman and Roman houses in Italy. Almost a decade ago he suggested that I study the house architecture at I Faraglioni as part of my dissertation. Ross encouraged me to think about the human experience of houses, inspiring me to venture into theoretical issues that are prominent in this paper and elsewhere. All translations are based on Loeb Classical Library editions unless otherwise noted.

Frequently used abbreviations:

Bakker 1994. J. Bakker, Living and Working with the Gods (Amsterdam, Gieben).

Bourdieu 1977. P. Bourdieu, Outline of a Theory of Practice (Cambridge, Cambridge University Press).

Clarke 1991. J. Clarke, Houses of Roman Italy, 100 BC – AD 250 (Berkeley, University of California Press).

Flower 1997. H. Flower, Ancestral Masks and Aristocratic Power in Roman Culture (Oxford, Oxford University Press).

Rawson, B. (ed.), 1991. Marriage, Divorce and Children in Ancient Rome (Oxford, Oxford University Press).

Rawson, B. and P. Weaver, 1997 (eds.). The Roman Family in Italy (Oxford, Clarendon Press).

Saller 1994. R. Saller, in Patriarchy, Property and Death in the Roman Family (Cambridge, Cambridge University Press).

Wallace-Hadrill 1994. A. Wallace-Hadrill, Houses and Society in Pompeii and Herculaneum (Princeton, Princeton University Press).

## Introduction

Ancestors engaged the living on many levels in Roman houses, capable of protecting or harming, providing moral and social benefits. They were represented visually in the atrium and other semi-public spaces by death masks, shield portraits, busts and written records of their achievements. Ancestral images were essential components of the system of social reproduction during the Republic, ensuring the continuity of family position through the generations. Social reproduction is the system that guides the passage of a family from one generation to the next. Social reproductive strategies are employed by the parental generation in the interest of maintaining cultural values and improving the social position of the family unit. Marriage strategies, reproduction, inheritance and socialization of children all contribute to this process. Bourdieu's habitus model of social reproduction examines how children internalize cultural principles and structures in the home.[1] Although ideal rules for behavior exist, frameworks of competing expectations regulate social activity. Through practice, children become accustomed to certain patterns and rhythms of activity and meaning. Building a bank of experience one event at a time, each person develops habits and values that guide behavior. A member of the community may choose to apply certain rules and ignore others depending on the particular situation. In fact, fulfilling all of the social "rules" which apply to a given situation is almost never possible.[2] Saller illustrates this kind of process in his recent study of the use of domestic rituals and dress in the service of reproducing power relationships through the generations. He shows that the systematic differentiation between free and enslaved members of the house with respect to punishments, dress and place in household rituals caused the power structures of Roman society to be internalized by all members of the household. The resulting power structure, highly unfair from our perspective, was accepted as natural by Romans, exploiters and exploited alike.[3]

---

[1] See Bourdieu 1977 and R. Blanton, Houses and Households: A Comparative Study, 1994, for discussion of how this process relates to domestic settings and case studies drawn from a range of cultures.

[2] Bourdieu 1977.

The ancestors were most influential in the reproduction of an ideology supporting elite families. Emphasis on descent and ancestral achievement provided a powerful check on social mobility during the Republican period. Fundamental changes in the relationship of self to the community of ancestors complicated the use of ancestral imagery in the later Republic and early Empire. As the Republican core of elite families came to play a smaller role in politics and society, the meanings of the images they had used to reinforce their elite positions were transformed. The influence of ancestral images on life in the house became problematic, and may have affected house design as well as social conventions. The atrium was the center of sacred activity in a Republican house, especially with respect to ancestors. The atrium-centered domus may have become less effective (and so, less popular) as the meanings of domestic ancestral representation changed in the wake of the civil war and proscriptions of the first c. BCE. Wallace-Hadrill emphasizes that theatrical presentation was an appealing feature of peristyle houses popular in Imperial times.[4] Potential for dramatic presentation could certainly have been a factor that conditioned the selection of new kinds of houses, as more freedmen and others from non-senatorial backgrounds came to play a larger role in politics at all levels.

These and other aspects of family life were in a constant state of change and tension. Old symbols took on new meanings and roles as needs changed. As wealth and personal contacts replaced family history and respectability as principal determinants of social standing, a more indexical framework of representation came to predominate over the traditional canonical system. Indexical communication emphasizes the economic standing of a member within a community, while canonical emphasizes conformity to shared norms. The former is typical of complex urban societies with open access to enfranchisement whereas the latter is more typical of closed traditional communities in which the residential group is stable and behavior can be closely monitored.[5] Such transformations are often observed in societies in transition from a closed membership to an expanding one.[6] In Rome, as more "new men" entered the upper ranks of Roman society, horizontal social connections and current economic position superseded vertical genealogies as the primary attributes of status.[7]

The sources pertinent to the study of ancestors in ancient Roman houses are problematic, yielding an incomplete and rather inconsistent picture.[8] The relevant literary evidence has many chronological gaps, especially before the mid-first century BCE. This situation means that too much emphasis is often placed on later sources as evidence for earlier periods. Many sources are difficult to assess because authors romanticized the past, exploiting it as a source of moral exempla for their contemporaries. The archaeological data are also biased, but in different ways. Our richest evidence for domestic architecture in Roman Italy comes from the Bay of Naples and the city of Ostia. These sites have yielded valuable information on many aspects of houses, including domestic cult.[9] Nevertheless, each is rather limited in chronological terms, the former having been sealed in the late first century CE and the latter having flourished during the second. Ancestral images took on more varied roles and the conventions governing their use were more relaxed in the early empire.

---

[3] R. Saller, The hierarchical household in Roman society: a study of domestic slavery, in M. Bush ed., Serfdom and Slavery, in press. Also see Saller, Corporal Punishment, Authority and Obedience in the Roman Household, in B. Rawson ed., Marriage, Divorce and Children in Ancient Rome, 1991: p. 144–65. M. George has raised many related issues in "Repopulating the Roman House," in Rawson and Weaver 1997: p. 299–319.

[4] A. Wallace-Hadrill, Houses and Society in Pompeii and Herculaneum, 1994, p. 51–52

[5] Blanton 1994, cit. n.1, p. 8 ff.

[6] Ibidem.

[7] For the most recent discussion of this problem, see Saller cit. in note 3: ch. 4. Also see R. Saller, "Familia, Domus and the Roman Conception of the Family," Phoenix 38, 1984, p. 336–55; Y. Thomas,"Mariages endogamiques à Rome. Patrimonie, pouvoir et parenté depuis l'époque archaïque," RD 58, 1980, p. 345–82.

[8] The chronological difficulties inherent to the data often force us to speak in generalities – "early Republican", "Republican", "Imperial" and so on. This should not be taken to imply that the transformation of the Roman political superstructure had an immediate direct effect on processes of social reproduction. It is merely an unfortunate consequence of our lack of chronological control.

[9] Important new studies of domestic cult in Roman houses include Bakker 1994 and T. Frölich, Lararien und Fassenbilder in den Vesuvustadten. Studien zur volkstumlichen pompejanischen Malerei RM Supp. 32, 1991, J. Bakker 1994.

The material assemblages from the houses of Campania and Ostia reflect later usage, making the reconstruction of first c. BCE contexts difficult. A further and more serious difficulty is social. Few houses from these sites were occupied by leading families with distinguished genealogies and large collections of ancestral imagines.[10] Even those houses that were owned by senatorial families were not their primary residences, and did not necessarily conform to the norms as expressed in the literary sources. A study emphasizing social reproduction must be sensitive to the different kinds of social relationships that were reproduced in different kinds of households.

Deficiencies in the literary and archaeological data have misled scholars into thinking about Roman houses and domestic settings in terms of well-defined types. Neither literary nor archaeological evidence suggests that the idea of a house was static over space, time or class. A more productive way to think about houses would be to think of them as embedded in dynamic systems of social, ideological and behavioral practice.[11] As patterns of behavior and ideology changed over space and time, the needs served by houses changed as well. Attitudes about family structure through the generations changed profoundly over the 2nd/1st c. BCE. These changes were reflected in the strategies for self-representation of people of various classes, in the relationship of families to particular houses, and in the spatial relationship between the living and the dead. Elaborate town houses were mostly organized

around an atrium during the late Republic and early Empire,[12] but innovative forms, like large peristyles and multiple atria, were not rare in first c. BCE Pompeii.[13] At Ostia in the 2nd c. CE almost no canonical atrium houses were in use.[14]

## Ancestors as examples for emulation

The community of ancestors was an important means of maintaining social order and demanding high standards of behavior. Their images, in the semi-public space of the atrium, stood as a reminder to the visitors of a great house that the present generation was held to a high standard of conduct. The imagines not only advertised the past deeds of a family, but guaranteed future achievement and sobriety. This mechanism seems to have been particularly effective during the Republican period. As the imagines came to be used in multiple communicative frameworks, incorporating indexical as well as canonical concerns, their moral role became more problematic. A well-known passage from Sallust illustrates the power that ancestral images were thought to have had before the first c. BCE.

> I have often heard that Quintus Maximus, Publius Scipio and other eminent men of our country, were in the habit of declaring that their hearts were set mightily aflame for the pursuit of virtue whenever they gazed on the masks of their ancestors. Of course they did not mean to imply that the wax or the effigy (figuram) had any such power over them, but rather it is the memory of great deeds that kindles in the breasts of noble men this flame that cannot be quelled until they by their own prowess have equaled the fame and glory of their forefathers.
>
> Sallust, Bell. Jug. IV.5

Sallust's description of the moral force exerted by the imagines over the members of great Republican families may seem a bit romanticized, but it finds echoes in other

---

[10] There are, of course, a few exceptions, such as the houses associated with the Poppaei, such as the villa at Oplontus or the Casa del Menandro. See M. della Corte, Case e abitanti di Pompei, 1965, Flower 1997, p. 42–43.

[11] Social and behavioral approaches to Roman domestic architecture have become common in recent years, due in large measure to the important contributions of A. Wallace-Hadrill. See especially his The Social Structure of the Roman House, PBSR 56, 1988, p. 43–97 and Wallace-Hadrill 1994. Other important studies on the relationship of social life to houses include Clarke 1991 and E. Dwyer, The Pompeian Atrium House in Theory and Practice, in E. Gazda (ed.), Roman Art in the Private Sphere, 1991, p. 25–48. Recent dissertations that treat material residues and social-behavioral practice include P. Foss, Kitchens and Dining Rooms at Pompeii: the spatial and social relationship of cooking to eating in the Roman household 1994 and P. Allison, The Distribution of Pompeian House Contents and its Significance 1992. See P. Allison, Artefact Distribution and Spatial Function in Pompeian Houses, in Rawson and Weaver eds., 1997, p. 321–54.

[12] Dwyer, cit. in note 11.

[13] Well-known examples of houses with multiple atria include the Casa del Fauno (VI.xii.2/5) and the Casa del Argenteria (VI.vii.20–22). The great peristyles of the Casa del Fauno and the Casa di Pansa (VI.vi.1) manifest the same concerns with display and opulence that eventually lead to the later popularity of peristyle based domestic architecture, but maintain the atrium, still important as the core of a house.

[14] Bakker 1994.

backward looking works of the late Republic and early Empire. Flower has emphasized the role of the imagines as an audience, watching over the behavior of the living. The imagines bore the burden of potential shame and conferred the social benefit of conspicuous honor.[15] The story of T. Manlius Torquatus (mid-second c. BCE), who demanded that his son leave the house for taking bribes (the son subsequently committed suicide) exemplifies similar ancestral power. Torquatus was spurred on to this severe judgement by the image of Torquatus Imperiosus, notorious for his severity, and the family's imagines and tituli.[16]

> The son's shameful death might have deflected some of the father's sternness. But he took no part in the mourning for his son, and at the very moment of the funeral he made himself available to clients who came to him for legal advice. For he saw that he was seated in the same atrium as Torquatus Imperiosus, notorious for his severity (see Livy, VIII.7); and Torquatus the lawyer remembered that the purpose of the custom of placing the images of one's ancestors and their tituli in the front part of the house was precisely so that their descendants should . . . imitate their deeds.

> Valerius Maximus, V.8
> (Gardner and Wiedemann trans.)

Imagines had a powerful impact on citizens like Torquatus and his visitors. Another important function of the imagines was to provide examples of virtuous behavior for the children in the house. Polybius related the most explicit surviving statement about the importance of the imagines in the training of the young during the mid-second century BCE.

> There could not be a more ennobling spectacle for a young man who aspires to fame and virtue. For who would not be inspired by the sight of the images of men renowned for their excellence, all together and as if alive and breathing? What spectacle could be more glorious than this?

> Polybius VI.53

Processions of ancestral images, at funerals or at celebrations of major family achievements must have had a powerful impact on the children in the house. Even when the imagines were just hanging on the wall, or closed within their cupboards, they and their tituli must have instilled a powerful fascination in the children of the house. Children may also have learned by participating in or imitating the activities and rituals performed by adults.[17] Of course, the free-born aristocratic children and the dependent alumni and vernae would have been keenly aware of their respective positions within the familia, their roles in rituals and their relationships with the imagines.[18] Boys and girls would have recognized differences in the gender specific messages with which a traditional atrium was furnished. The loom would have been one important focus of women's (and girls') attention, as attested in many literary sources.[19] The imagines may not have been exclusively related to the agnatic line, however, since a woman's imagines could accompany her to her new home when she married.[20] Cicero cites the virtue of the women of gens Claudia as paragons of virtue (and as witnesses to the shame of their descendants) in a manner very similar to the tone seen in references to male ancestors.[21]

In references to use in the Imperial period, many authors played on the irony that corrupt individuals displayed ancestral images as status symbols, in contrast to their traditional meanings. Imagines seem to have remained symbols of high social position, although in practice their moral purpose may have been subverted. Pliny the Elder cited a speech by the orator M. Valerius Messala Corvinus (cos. 31 BC) and the treatise on families by M.

---

[15] Flower 1997, p. 12–15.

[16] This passage is often cited to exemplify the sternness of Roman fathers in general: J. Gardner and T. Wiedemann, eds., trans., The Roman Household: A Sourcebook, 1991. This position has been criticized persuasively by Saller, 1994.

[17] The importance of children's participation in ritual and social obligations in children's socialization is discussed in B. Rawson, Adult-Child Relationship in Roman Society, in Rawson ed., 1991, p. 7–30 (esp. p. 18–19).

[18] Saller, cit. in note 3 and forthcoming.

[19] The association of women and wool working are many, including women of all classes. Conspicuous examples of patrician women working wool in the atrium include Lucretia (Livy, I.57.9) and Asconius 43C (see Flower 1996: 194); also see A. Wallace-Hadrill, Engendering the Roman House, in D. Kleiner and S. Matheson eds., I Claudia. Women in Ancient Rome, 1996, p. 104–15.

[20] Flower, 1997: p. 212–13 cites Maecenas' display of his wife's ancestors among his family tree, citing Prop. 3.19 and Horace, Carm. 3.29.1.

[21] Cicero, Pro Caelio 34.

Valerius Messala Rufus (cos. 53 BC) to illustrate the rigorous exclusivity observed during republican times in displaying ancestral images.[22] Messala the younger was protesting against a relative who had placed a bust of the Laevini among the family imagines, while Messala the elder was objecting to the Salvittiones claiming a false connection to the Scipios. These complaints show that regard for the inviolability of the family was still maintained by some during the late Republic.[23] This respect for tradition stands out against the more promiscuous approach taken by many Romans in assembling sets of imagines from the first c. BCE onwards.[24]

The irony that many corrupt people had halls full of decaying but venerable images struck satirists and philosophers alike, as seen in the comments made by Juvenal and Seneca.[25] These authors emphasize the ideal message of the imagines, although in practice the meanings of the imagines have been complicated. We must be wary of the distortions that these writers were likely to have built into their images of the Republic. They constructed a past that stood in moral opposition to the present. From Sallust to Juvenal this rhetorical device was employed for centuries. Nevertheless, written sources consistently stressed the importance of descent and civic achievement for families of high rank during Republican times.[26] During Imperial times Romans clearly continued to use busts of purported ancestors in the creation of images of themselves. Many people were impressed by the inclusion of lots of famous statues among the imagines of the wealthy and powerful. Nevertheless, these images had taken on properties beyond the moral and spiritual aspects stressed most frequently in earlier times. In some cases, they became a kind of collectible curiosity, which could be bought and sold as commodities.[27] The great fire of 64 CE destroyed many

old houses decorated with Republican war trophies and imagines, depriving many families that still used them according to custom.[28] The effect may have been to reduce the traditional usage of ancestral images, reinforcing their antique (as opposed to traditional) value.

## How were the dead used in the construction of an idea of family?

In Republican times the dead were considered a significant part of the domestic unit. Polybius, who witnessed and described Roman funerary processions in the mid-Republic, provides our most reliable account of the use of ancestral images in pre-Gracchan Rome.[29] The rituals described by Polybius VI.53 are notable not only for the light they shed on funerary practices in Rome at an early date, but also for the diachronic notion of family structure which is emphasized. Eminent living and deceased representatives of the family attended events of major public importance.[30] The processions of ancestors marking accession to public office appear to have been discontinued at some point in the late Republic, since the practice appears to have been considered antique by the time of Tiberius:

> [Tiberius] highly complimented a praetor, because on entering upon his office he had revived the ancient custom of eulogising his ancestors before the people.
>
> Suetonius, Tib. 32

Suetonius characterizes ancestral processions marking achievement of high office as ancient[31] with reference to Tiberius' lifetime, citing it as one of several actions cited that showed the emperor's high moral standards early in his career. The passage contrasts with the passage from Polybius cited above, in which such processions were pre-

---

[22] See Flower 1997, p. 58–9 for discussion.

[23] Pliny, NH XXXV.ii.

[24] A little later in the passage Pliny himself excuses the appropriation of images of virtuous non-relatives, as showing admiration for their virtues. Also see Cicero, Epist. Ad Fam., IX.21.2–3. Flower 1997: 291 disputes Shackleton Bailey's (Cicero: Epistulae ad Familiares, 1977) assertion that Cicero is joking in this letter.

[25] Juvenal VIII.1–9, 19–21 on Ponticus not living up to the imagines on display in his home; Seneca, De Benef. III.28.2 remarks that imagines do not make a person noble.

[26] Saller cit. in note 7.

[27] Note Pliny XXV.4: "ipsi honorem non nisi in pretio ducentes, ut frangat heres furisque detrahat laqueus." Of course, if imagines could be stolen and sold, some degree of detachable value must have been ascribed to them in addition to the traditional symbolic value they had always possessed.

[28] Suetonius, Nero 38.2; Tacitus, Ann. XV.xli.

[29] Polybius, VI.53.

[30] Including the undertaking of public sacrifices and magistracies as well as funerals.

[31] "consuetudinem antiquam retulisset."

sented as contemporary and ordinary practice among the elite. The deep intergenerational structure of the family and its achievements is highlighted in Polybius as an especially praiseworthy element of Roman tradition. The persistent focus on the male line, and male activities might be dismissed as reflecting the gender bias of the author and his Greek audience, but it is consistent with the emphasis on civic achievement seen in other republican references.

Ancestral images continued to be used among the highest circles in funerals of the early imperial period. Tacitus recalled the funeral of Drusus in 9 BCE, rich with ancestral images in contrast to the meager funeral of his son Germanicus only thirty years later.[32]

Elite funerals were politically charged, and imagines from the family of the deceased and allied lineages could accompany the procession. At the funeral of Iunia in 22 CE, imagines from twenty of the most illustrious families in Rome joined the parade honoring the niece of Cato the Younger, wife of C. Cassius and sister of M. Brutus. With a Republican pedigree like that, it is hardly surprising that Iunia's family sponsored a funeral in a grand old style. The accumulation of masks from as many prestigious clans as possible for a grand funeral can be seen as an indexical display of family connections within society. The display represented connections and power in a political arena, independent of the adherence to community standards. Such use of imagines is not likely to have begun in Imperial times, although it may have been promoted as part of a broader shift towards indexical forms of display.

Roman families are often thought to have become increasingly nuclear during the Imperial period, with less emphasis on vertical continuity. Some studies emphasize the promotion of conjugal bonds during the late Republic,[33] although generalizations about well-defined types of marital relationships are not easy to make.[34] For example, Saller has recently discussed the "diminution of the agnatic principle" in the early empire as a tool for self-promotion among the senatorial class. Families rose and fell into and out of prominence rapidly during this period. Few

senatorial families could boast a long and distinguished agnatic line.[35] Horizontal social connections, whether within the familia, domus, kin from either side of the nuclear family, patrons and friends, were much more important in Imperial Rome to the image of a prominent public figure. The demographic and economic expansion of the upper class diminished the importance of adhering to canonical principles in the pursuit of status. The public display of political power in funerary processions was an effective vehicle for the expression of family connections.

## Representation of ancestors in the home

Many types of sacred familial representations are known to have been used in Roman houses:[36] wax masks (imagines), shield portraits (clipeatae imagines), busts, written records of various kinds (tituli) and figures like the Lares, Genius and Dii Penates which had ancestral overtones but were not associated with particular ancestors. In general, greater care seems to have been exercised in assembling the body of ancestral images in Republican times, with a gradual weakening of traditional kinship requirements over time.[37] Pliny the Elder provides us with the most comprehensive discussion of imagines in ancient Rome.[38] He complained that painted portraits, which in the past had been very accurate representations, were no longer used. Bronze shields with silver images attached had become the preferred style, showcasing the wealth of the owners rather than their adherence to traditional values.[39] Heads of statues were exchanged for each other. People put up decorative statues of strangers, thinking more of the price than of family honors. He accused people of preferring to dis-

[32] Tacitus, Ann. III.v.

[33] S. Dixon, The Sentimental Ideal of the Roman Family, in B. Rawson ed., Marriage, Divorce and Children in Ancient Rome, 1991, p. 98–113.

[34] K. Bradley, Remarriage and Family Structure, in Rawson ed. 1991, p. 79–98.

[35] Saller, cit. in note 7, 1994.

[36] Recent studies of note include A. Gregory, Responses to Portraits and the Political Uses of Images in Rome, JRA 7 1994: p. 80–94. Also see G. Lahusen, Zur Funktion und Rezeption des Ahnenbildes, RM 92, 1985, p. 261–89.

[37] Saller, cit. in note 7, emphasized the sanctity of the familia as opposed to the more flexible domus. The agnatic familia played a much more important role in Republican politics, while the broader domus was more suitable to patronage systems under the emperors. Also, recall the story of Messala, cited above.

[38] Pliny, NH XXXV.4–14. This passage is frequently cited elsewhere, and will only be cited here with reference to specific details. See R. Winkes, Pliny's Chapter on Roman Funerary Customs in the Light of Clipeatae Imagines, AJA 83, 1979, p. 481–84 and Flower 1997: p. 302–6 for the complete text.

play athletic images in the "oiling-room" (ceromata) and Epicurus in the bedroom, celebrating his birthday and monthly festival in preference to those of the family. The use of rich materials and the collecting of images based on their artistic or intellectual merit point to the use of these portraits within an indexical communicative framework, strongly opposed to the canonical framework that dominated Pliny's characterization of Republican display.

> In the halls of our ancestors it was otherwise; portraits (imagines) were the objects displayed to be looked at, not statues (signa) by foreign artists nor bronzes nor marbles, but wax models of faces were set out, each on a separate side-board (armarium), to furnish likenesses to be carried in procession at a funeral in the clan, and always when some member of the clan passed away the entire company of his house that had ever existed was present. The pedigrees too were traced in a spread of lines running near the several painted portraits.[40] The archive rooms were kept filled with books of records with written memorials of official careers.[41] Outside the houses and round the doorways there were other presentations of those mighty spirits, with spoils taken from the enemy fastened to them, which even one who bought the house was not permitted to unfasten, and the mansions eternally celebrated a triumph even though they changed their masters. This acted as a mighty incentive, when every day even the very walls reproached an unwarlike owner with intruding on the triumphs of another…

> Pliny, NH XXXV.6–7

## Masks

Literary sources preserve a wealth of information about the use of imagines in the house and the ancestral processions associated with funerals and family celebrations.[42] They were fashioned of wax in a realistic representation of the subject, most likely during the sitter's lifetime.[43] No actual ancestral masks have been excavated, a problem

that has led to considerable confusion about their form and display. The literary sources consistently emphasize that the production of these masks was associated with the achievement of high office, even during the empire. Although the imagines of a woman's family might be used in her new home, there are no indications that masks of women were ever produced. The gender exclusivity of the type contrasts with portraiture in other media, such as painting and sculpture.[44] Masks were used to portray public achievement in the house, in a more private context than many other representations of ancestors. The cupboards that held imagines were normally kept closed.[45] Their presence could be felt at the salutatio, and identities read off the labels, but the images themselves were hidden. The tradition of keeping the imagines in closed cupboards must have enhanced their effectiveness when the doors were thrown open during times of celebration or mourning.

Few examples are known of imagines being kept in public places. Scipio Africanus' imago was taken down from the Capitol for Cornelian funerals, as was Cato's from the Senate, but otherwise the masks appear to have been associated with domestic contexts.[46] Appian contrasted Scipio's imago, placed in the temple of Jupiter with the storage of other masks in the forum. The implications of this statement are not clear, but it is possible that by the second half of the second century CE many masks were in state possession.[47]

---

[39] In contrast to Pliny's statement, R. Winkes, Clipeata Imago, 1969, a catalogue of shield portraits, shows about 4% of surviving examples to be of metal, none of which were from Italy. Once again, we have to be careful of using Pliny uncritically, given his clear moralistic objectives.

[40] "stemmata vero lineis discurrebant ad imagines pictas."

[41] "tabulina codicibus implebantur et monimentis rerum in magistratu gestarum."

[42] Flower 1997 has collected over 100 literary references dating from the second century BCE to the sixth century A.D. that refer to imagines. She argues that in the absence of a modifier or a context that suggests otherwise, "imagines" were the wax masks hung on the walls of atria and carried in processions. See Flower 1997, ch. 2 for a discussion of the form of the imagines.

[43] Flower 1997, p. 37–38.

[44] Flower 1997, p. 79.

[45] Flower 1997, p. 208–9.

[46] Appian, Iberica 89; Val. Max. 8.15.1

[47] Flower, 1997, p. 263 interprets this passage to imply that the Cornelii continued to use their imagines in funerals to that late date. The passage itself is ambiguous, and when the location of the others is considered, a more consistent reading would see the masks in the possession of the state. Flower does remark, however, that in the sources later than Appian the imagines are only associated with imperial funerals.

## *Shield Portraits (clipeatae imagines)*

The evidence for shield portraits in ancient Rome derives from both material and literary sources. Unfortunately, archaeological documentation for them, in the form of in-situ examples of real shield portraits, is wholly lacking. We know that during the republican period portraits of deceased ancestors painted, sculpted or attached to shields were hung high on the walls of the atria of elite families.[48] These portraits had strong civic and military associations, and were essential components of the representation of family history in the home. Unlike masks, however, from early republican times shield portraits were mounted on public monuments, like the Temple of Bellona and the Basilica Aemilia.[49] They may have been used in the home to evoke the grandeur of public settings, one of a range of forms and motives used by architects to convey a sense of monumentality.[50] The extant material evidence for shield portraits is restricted to the sculpted and painted representations of them in houses, public spaces and funerary monuments.[51] Painted representations were found in domestic contexts from the first century BCE until at least the second century CE. Examples have been found in the villa of Poppaea at Oplontis, the House of the Vettii and the House of the Impluvium.[52] In the villa at Oplontis, the clipeate images were set within an elaborate and colorful second style context, part of a dazzling show that overwhelmed the viewer rather than evoking a traditional atrium with its ancestral monuments.[53] Note too, that the simple wax masks of ancestors were missing, although we might expect them in an atrium filled with shield portraits. The use of clipeate images in triclinium 14 of the

same villa was still further removed from the traditional uses of ancestral images in the house. The painted shields hung within a temple precinct, set among jeweled columns and fanciful architecture.[54] These images were not reproductions of clipeate images in the elite houses of Rome. They are part of a decorative language designed to evoke public settings, in an opulent framework suitable for indexical displays. The gens Poppaea was wealthy and connected in Rome, including two consuls in 9 CE and Poppaea Sabina, wife of Nero.[55] Presumably, the houses that this family owned in Rome would have been adorned with imagines. Oplontis was a different setting, though, where different kinds of competition raged. The canonical framework of expression maintained in the formal aristocratic houses in Rome was less influential in Oplontis.

The clipeate images painted on the walls of townhouses in Pompeii did not conform to the traditional norms any more that those of the villa at Oplontis. The images in the House of the Beautiful Impluvium (I.ix.1) were set in the tablinum, as might be expected. But they too were set in an elaborate architectural fantasy rather than a representation of a proper atrium.[56] The clipeatae imagines from the House of the Great Altar (VI.xvi.15) are depicted on the back wall of the atrium, again as we might expect, but they are shown together with actors' masks, in a theatrical fantasy.[57] The clipeatae imagines from the House of the Vettii (VI.xv.1) are depicted in triclinium p, facing onto the peristyle. These have almost no relationship to their traditional antecedents, framing the dramatic scenes of Dionysos and Ariadne and Daedalus and Pasiphae.[58] The prestigious yet unelaborated wax masks of ancestors are not associated with any of these painted representations, nor with tituli explaining identity. None of these examples is an actual shield portrait. In fact, the faces depicted are all idealized, excluding the possibility that they were portraits. The Campanian shield portraits are all decorative fancy, plays on the traditional aesthetic of placing

---

[48] Vitruvius VI.iii.6.

[49] Pliny (NH XXXV.12) comments that Appius Claudius had placed a set of his family clipeate images in the temple of Bellona in 495 BCE. Possibly one of his later namesakes was responsible for placing the images in the temple (Appius Claudius Caecus or Appius Claudius Pulcher, cos. 79 BCE). On public use of clipeate portraits see G. Sauron, Quis Deum? (Rome 1994): 62–78.

[50] Vitruvius VI.iii.6, 8–9; Wallace-Hadrill 1994, p. 7–37; Clarke 1991: 237; F. Coarelli, Architettura sacra e architettura privata nella tarda repubblica, Architecture et Société (Coll.Ec.Fr.Rom. 66) p. 191–217.

[51] Winkes, cit. in note 39.

[52] Winkes, cit. in note 38.

[53] Clarke 1991, p. 113–14.

[54] A. DeFranciscis, The Pompeian Wall Paintings in the Roman Villa at Oplontis, 1975, p. 12, pl. 17.

[55] Flower 1997, p. 42–43.

[56] For illustrations, see Winkes, cit. in note 38, pl. 68 or R. Ling, Roman Painting, 1991, fig. 168.

[57] For illustration, see I. Baldassare (ed.), Pompei. Pitture e Mosaici. vol. V (Regio VI, parte seconda), 1994, p. 853–55.

[58] Ibidem, p. 537.

shield portraits high on the walls of public buildings as well as the atria of aristocratic houses.

The decline of the so-called First style of wall painting in the early first c. BCE was part of a group of changes in the domestic advertisement of status. The First style provided a restrained, formal background against which family trophies could be showcased. The more decorative characteristics of the Second style created an opulent stage on which the patron might operate, highly differentiated in terms of quality and expense, and so suited to the indexical display of wealth.[59] After the demise of the First style, the clipeata imago became one of many decorative elements that might be chosen by a wall painter. It is interesting that most of the examples belong to the first c. CE, several generations removed from the decline of the domestic shield portrait tradition.

Clipeatae imagines could also be represented on sculpture: in stone too the type lost much of its traditional exclusivity during the empire. In public contexts clipeate images clearly retained many of their ancestral and honorific functions, although the gender specificity of the Republican series was not maintained.[60] Clipeate portraits and their derivatives became popular on the private burial monuments of the middle class during imperial times.[61] One of the most interesting of the funerary reliefs depicting clipeatae imagines is the "Testamentum Relief" in the Capitoline museum, the focus of a new study by D'Ambra.[62] The relief evokes a Roman atrium during the funeral of a young man. A clipeate male portrait watches over a youth reclining between a seated matron and a slave counting on an abacus. Presumably the relief represents the funeral of the young man, whose deceased father and living mother mourn him.[63] The relief was mounted on the façade of a tomb, establishing an implicit link between domestic space and the grave. Using traditional aristocratic images, middle class patrons attempted to clothe themselves in elite Republican dignity. But at the same time, the shallow genealogy represented typifies middle class imperial society. They constitute a nuclear family: the clipeate male figure is no Torquatus Imperiosus, several generations removed, but a grieving and grieved-for husband and father. Many other clipeate images from first–second c. CE funerary monuments are employed in roughly the same way: to honor a deceased loved one, rather than to perpetuate the memory of family achievement.[64] This change in usage is part of a broader trend in which many traditional images associated with the Republican aristocracy were employed in a broader range of social contexts. Busts, inscriptions, dress and shield portraits were all adopted by the upwardly-mobile middle class to express their new prosperity and ambition.[65]

## Ancestral Busts and Statues

Portrait busts and statues of the deceased were a third important mode of commemorating the ancestors in the house, for which there is physical and literary evidence. Two elaborate shrines were found in the House of the Menander in Pompeii (I.x.4), a well-preserved Republican house of the Poppaei, a leading local family.[66] A group of small busts in a perishable material (most likely wax) were

[59] Wallace-Hadrill 1994, p. 143–74 has developed a ranking of opulence for wall painting based on color choice (167), elaboration of structure and design, and fineness of finish. All of these elements could be used to represent and interpret the costliness of a given room.

[60] Note the spectacular bust of Agrippina Minor among the clipeata imagines in Trajan's Forum, now on display in the Markets. See S. Wood, Memoriae Agrippinae: Agrippina the Elder in Julio-Claudian Art and Propaganda, AJA 92, 1988, p. 409–26 (p. 424–25).

[61] D. Kleiner, Roman Imperial Funerary Altars with Portraits 1987. See the large collection of clipeate and related images presented by D. Scarpellini, Stele romane con imagines clipeatae in Italia, 1987. I thank E. D'Ambra for this last reference.

[62] E. D'Ambra, "Mourning and the Making of Ancestors in the Testamentum Relief," AJA 99, 1995, p. 667–81.

[63] Ibidem, fig. 1. D'Ambra cites Trimalchio's banquet (Petronius, Sat. 78) as evidence for propping the dead up at funerals. A. Zadoks-Jitta thought that models were used rather than the deceased themselves (Ancestral Portraiture in Rome, Amsterdam 1932).

[64] D'Ambra, cit. in note 63, notes the parallel to the use of busts to indicate loved ones who had predeceased commemorands in kline monuments from Rome and London.

[65] For examples of economically rising classes using the imagery of the former elite in the expression of status via funerary practices, see A. Cannon, The Historical Dimension in Mortuary Expressions of Status and Sentiment, Current Anthropology 30.4, 1989, p. 437–58. Cannon cites essentially the same cycle of middle class emulation of elite practices followed by elite adoption of new practices in Victorian England, historical Iroquoia and ancient Greece.

[66] Clarke 1991, p. 170.

set up on a shrine looking onto the peristyle. The busts are not well enough preserved for us to examine their features. Given their humble material and form, we can assume that they were ancestral portraits rather than fancy statues of philosophers or writers that were popular collectibles from the first c. BCE onwards. The form of these images (busts rather than masks) and their placement by the peristyle rather than the atrium contrast strikingly with the expectations we might have from the literary sources examined above. These findings are, however, consistent with those from other houses and sites that indicate a strong link between household cult and peristyles.[67]

The Forum of Augustus in Rome must have had a powerful impact on the way that portrait statues were perceived by the population of Rome. The portraits of leading figures from Roman history were all assembled in the gallery of summi viri, like the imagines for the entire city of Rome. The most distinguished members of all the great families were displayed as full-length statues in the forum, together with tituli in a vast paraphrase of a traditional atrium.[68] Like Torquatus and the other patricians watched over by their family imagines, Augustus was held accountable by the summi viri.[69] The honorary statue of Augustus in a triumphal quadriga dominated the center of the forum, like a patron in his tablinum. It is intriguing to speculate that the open space of the forum might have inspired homeowners like the Poppaei to display ancestral images along peristyles, in a quotation of the latest, most splendid of Rome's architectural wonders.

### Family archives

Our evidence for the kinds of written records kept about ancestral careers is scant. That such records were kept is indisputable, given the literary testimony.[70] Clearly, the portraits displayed in the atrium were furnished with genealogical and biographical information. Unfortunately,

the precise form of the records kept in the archives remains a mystery. Lists of tituli and achievements must have been included among the family records. It is quite possible that historians had access to records of this sort, given that Livy complained on a number of occasions about families doctoring the records of the deceased kept with their imagines. The practice dates back to at least the mid-fifth c. BCE, when the descendants of L. Minucius falsified an inscription on his portrait ("falsum imaginis titulum"), claiming he was a tribunus plebis.[71] Centuries later, the descendants of Q. Fabius Maximus claimed he was "dictator" rather than "acting dictator."[72] A more general statement of exasperation shows that the practice was not unusual:[73]

> It is not easy to choose between the accounts or the authorities. The records have been vitiated, I think, by funeral eulogies and by lying inscriptions under portraits, every family endeavoring mendaciously to appropriate victories and magistracies to itself – a practice which has certainly wrought confusion in the achievements of individuals and in the public memorials of events...

> Livy, VIII.xl.4–5

Livy's complaint is valuable for several reasons. First, it assigned a certain amount of responsibility for maintaining and publishing records about individual achievements to families. This must be related to the written records kept in the family archives. Second, it attests the Republican emphasis on family achievement as an essential component of inter-family competition in a critical rather than a romanticizing context. Third, the link between imagines and textual documentation is assumed, showing our modern distinctions between the two to be arbitrary.

The two editions of the epitaph of Scipio Barbatus shed interesting light on the problem of 'updating' epi-

---

[67] Clarke 1991, p. 7 makes the intriguing suggestion that portable altars may have been used for ancestral sacrifices. This would allow for a continuation of ancestral rituals in the atrium without any permanent architectural features.

[68] P. Zanker, Forum Augustum: das Bildnisprogramm, 1968, Flower 1997, p. 224–36.

[69] Suetonius, Augustus 31; P. Zanker, Power of Images in the Age of Augustus, 1988, p. 214.

[70] Flower 1997, ch. 5–6.

[71] Livy, IV.xvi.2–4.

[72] Livy, XXII.xxxi.10–11.

[73] J.P. Small, Artificial Memory and the Writing Habits of the Literate, Helios 22 1995, p. 159–66 and P. Culham, Documents and Domus in Republican Rome, Libraries and Culture 26 1991, p. 119–34 both emphasize the relatively flexible ancient concept of remembering, which generally tolerated errors which did not distort the gist of what was being remembered. In theory, however, the recording of careers was taken more seriously.

taphs in the interest of family propaganda, particularly, since the later edition represented his career inaccurately.[74] As competition for status in the late Republic intensified, families must have come under pressure to embellish the careers of distant ancestors, to distinguish them in comparison to more recent competitors. If Barbatus' epitaph was written about a century after his death, this was beyond the limits of human memory. Whether or not the expanded text is accurate, the practice of 'modernizing' or 'updating' epitaphs, public inscriptions and family archives may have led to precisely the kinds of distortions about which Livy was complaining.

## Concluding remarks:

Several changes in the Roman approach to ancestors in elite houses should be clear. First, the perception of chronological depth with respect to the family declined. This process most likely began in Republican times, gaining momentum in the chaotic post-Gracchan period. By the second c. CE the maintenance of long agnatic genealogical records had lost nearly all of its former relevance. Those who appeared to maintain such traditions might be praised by conservatives like Tiberius, or criticized by satirists like Seneca if they did not measure up to the standards set by their ancestors.

Ancestral images took on a much greater range of meanings as evaluation of family success and prestige came to be seen in more indexical terms. Indexical communication promoted a greater emphasis on expenditure, magnificence and decorativeness than had been the case before the first c. BCE. Evocation of public monuments, iconography and architectural contexts became fashionable in the empire, especially in the wake of Augustus's reign.[75] This trend was manifest in the use of clipeate images on the wall painting of dining halls, and the furnishing of the houses themselves.[76] The wide diffusion of many types of images that had, according to tradition, been reserved for the elite should be seen within this framework. The depiction of a freedman in a clipeata ima-

go should not be seen as the usurpation of the status traditionally conferred on the subject of such honor, rather it is an attempt to render an image in an esteemed public format. Wax masks of ancestors are not among the forms imitated by freedmen and other wealthy non-patricians, perhaps in part because of the low value of the medium. The low estimation of the cost of wax imagines would have made them unsuitable for indexical display. Portraits were used mostly in the cemeteries rather than the homes in the competition for status among the middle class residents of Rome. This probably reflects the more private nature of a middle class home, as opposed to the public nature of a patrician one.[77]

The transformation of ancestral representation in the house was not a purely chronological process. Certainly the social mobility of the middle class was a factor. As commoners and freedmen rose into the ranks of the powerful in Rome, their notions of family and value systems were passed on to their children and diffused into the upper classes. Their social mobility contributed to a sense of instability that undermined the traditional systems of evaluation based on ancestral achievement. Republican families, particularly in the pre-Gracchan period, were judged by their adherence to a system of canonical rules. Ancestral images provided a moral structure for behavior, and guaranteed high expectations for members of the great houses. These images and the rigid codes of behavior they represented were transformed in the later Republic and Empire.

The focus of domestic worship spread beyond the atrium, depriving it of its traditional meaning within a canonical communicative framework. With the decreased emphasis on ancestral ritual and representation, there was less reason to design elite dwellings around such a modest architectural form. The new elite in Roman society needed houses that expressed fundamentally different sources of power, based on wealth and a wide network of social relations. In this context peristyle-based domus and elaborate luxury villas enjoyed great success and atria slowly disappeared.[78] The intimate links between ideas about family and house form underscore the importance of the

---

[74] For discussion see F. Coarelli, Il Sepolcreto degli Scipioni a Roma, 1988.

[75] Zanker, cit. in note 69, p. 265–95.

[76] Ibidem, p. 270–74 discusses the use of Augustan imagery in a range of domestic media, from bronze table stands to terracotta lamps.

[77] Vitruvius (VI.v.) remarked that commoners have no need of grand spaces that evoke public architecture because they do not have the same social requirements that patricians do.

[78] Bakker 1994, p. 27.

house as the locus for social reproduction. In the house, children learn the rules about power relationships, gender, privacy and the place of the dead in the family. Such rules are rarely followed to the letter – much of the recent scholarship on Roman families focuses on the inconsistency between ideals and practical realities.[79] Bourdieu's model of social process is especially useful in that it accounts for ideals, general tendencies and practical application at the same time. The house was bound to the social institutions and rules it was designed to reproduce.[80] The atrium was essential to houses of a certain social level until its sacred and ideological functions were transformed as part of a new approach to the representation and reproduction of social relationships. Changes in the representation of ancestors within the domestic setting allowed the transformation of the architectural forms that had structured the traditional domestic ideology.

---

[79] The essays on ancient Rome in Kertzer and Saller (eds.), The Family in Italy from Antiquity to the Present, 1991, provide a good idea of the sweep of such studies, ranging from sexuality and the law (Cohen) to kinship and marital strategies (Treggiari, Corbier) and the transmission of property (Saller).

[80] For a well documented ethnographic example of this kind of study, see P. Bourdieu, The Berber House, in M. Douglas (ed.), Rules and Meanings, 1973, p. 98–110.

# AUGUSTAN IMAGERY
# ON COINAGE FROM PAPHOS

*Catheryn Leda Cheal*

While working as a graduate student in the early 1970's, I was first encouraged and inspired for the study of ancient numismatics by the enthusiasm of R. Ross Holloway. Contrary to most archaeological inquirers of the time, he was interested in the meaning of imagery and why certain images were chosen. (R. Ross Holloway, A View of Greek Art, 1973.) Further study with the late Tony Hackens at the American Numismatic Society demonstrated the methods and possibilities of working with depictions of architecture on coins. (T. Hackens, Histoire et iconographie du temple capitolin de Rome et de la triade capitoline, (Diss. Unpub., 1962). I wish to thank both of these prominent archaeologists for their brilliant models of scholarship and kindly pedagogical encouragement.

---

The ubiquitous presence of coins is crucial for a society's view of itself, since its imagery intersects boundaries of politics, economics, religion, and social structures. The coins of Paphos, in particular, given their long history of development in antiquity with both deviations and conformity to Greek and Roman types, provide a glimpse into a local state's need for definition within the dominant Roman power. It was to the advantage of Eastern cities and the elite groups that controlled them to define their power and privileges in terms acceptable to the imperial court at Rome. And Rome, as well, needed provincial coinage types that clearly integrated local identification with the stability of the Roman Empire.

There are three major groups of ancient coins from the Paphian region of Cyprus – from the fifth century B.C., the Hellenistic period, and from Roman times. The Cinyrad dynasty of priest-kings from Old Paphos, whose personal names first appear on the coins in the Cypriote syllabary, minted coins in the fifth century B.C. Types primarily include bulls, eagles, and the astragali of Aphrodite.[1]

In the fourth century B.C., the mint production at Cyprus was under the supervision of the strategos, appointed by the Ptolemaic rulers of Egypt.[2] The head of Herakles and the full body of an enthroned Zeus are represented on coins during Alexander's rule. Later, portrait heads of Ptolemaic rulers, appropriate for the Hellenistic concept of ruler cults, are typical reverses, as well as a series with Zeus' eagle on one side and the head of Aphrodite on the other. (Fig. 1)

This paper is primarily concerned with the Roman series, in particular those coins showing the sanctuary of Aphrodite.[3] The series started with Augustus and was produced in Nea Paphos, about ten miles from the old city. Coins with the head of Augustus and a Nike have an inscription COC OCT(AV O) DESIG, and thus have been dated to post-27 B.C., when the provinces were partitioned and Augustus retained Cyprus. The first of the so-called "temple-type" coins at Paphos appear in Cyprus after 22 B.C. (Fig. 2) because the proconsul, A. Plautius, is named on them. This architectural type is better described

---

[1] G. Hill, Catalogue of the Greek Coins of Cyprus, repr. 1964, p. lxii–lxxx, p. 35–44. A. M. Burnett, Roman Provincial Coinage, 1992. This study was based on the Paphian coins from the collections of the major catalogues and the collection in the American Numismatic Society.

[2] I. Nicolaou and O. Morkholm, Paphos, A Ptolemaic Coin Hoard, v. i, 1976.

[3] The study of architecture on ancient coins and the need for a systematic collection and comparison of all possible representations has been realized since the 1909 article of H. Dressel, Das Iseum campense auf einer Munze des Vespasian, Sitz. Ber. Der Kgl. Preuss. Akad., 1909, v. 25, p. 640–648. Later authors to emphasize this point include D. Brown, Sanctuaries of Rome as Coin types, American Numismatic Society, Numismatic Notes and Monographs, 90, 1940, p. 42; B. Trell, The Sanctuary of Artemis at Ephesos, American Numismatic Society, Numismatic Notes and Monographs, 107, 1945; T. Hackens, Architectura Numismatica, a propos de quelques publications recentes, L'Antiquite Classique, 41, 1972, p. 245–254; K. Wulzinger, Die Macellum-Dupondien des Nero, Numismatik Internationale Monatsschrift, 2, 1933, p. 83–95 and p. 116–138; and A. Muehsam, Coin and Sanctuary. A Study of the Architectural Representations on Ancient Jewish Coins, Near Eastern Researches I, 1966.

as a sanctuary, since the gates more likely lead into an open-air courtyard than a building.[4] The Paphian sanctuary type consists of an aniconic stone (baetyl)[5] with the central architectural structure made of two tall, double-pointed piers joined by a cross beam, flanked by candelabra[6] and, in front, a semi-circular courtyard. These were the most important visual elements of the sanctuary, faithfully copied by the bronzes of Drusus, Galba, Vespasian, Titus, Trajan, and adapted by the silver coinage of Vespasian and the bronzes of the Severan family. Also remaining today are examples on bronze coins from Sardis and Pergamon, inscribed with "Paphia" for recognizability, and several gems and rings.[7]

It would be interesting to know for certain who was responsible for this choice of sanctuary imagery on the Augustan coins – the imperial court,[8] the governor and proconsul of Cyprus, A. Plautius, appointed by Augustus, or the local Paphian magistrates. From the time of Claudius, the Koinon Cyprion (Cyprian league), rather than an individual governor, is named on the coinage. While the extent of eastern local cities' or leagues' rights to mint coins and choose the denomination or image type varied throughout the imperial era and among different cities, it's quite clear that the emperor could grant or revoke minting privileges, especially under unusual political circumstances.[9] According to Cassius Dio (52.30.9), Augustus was advised by Maecenas to force the provinces to adopt Roman currencies and weights and measures, rather than keeping their own. Although such an ideal unity wasn't achieved, particularly in the East, it seems likely in the period of Augustus, at least, that cities didn't mint without the emperor's permission, since the state would have had control over the metal supply.[10] In the case of the Augustan coins from Paphos, coins with a reverse type of a Nike are a clear reference to Augustus' success. The portrait of Augustus was required by the imperial court, with definite similarities to sculptural portraits, particularly in the matter of agelessness.[11] While the responsibility of the choice of the sanctuary-type reverse, however, is not as clear, it is difficult to believe that the two sides of the coin were determined by entirely different processes, one imperial and one local.[12] Ultimately, however, Rome and Paphos were working towards the same goal: the authenticity of the coins as a means of stable exchange and a bond between the two political units based on the person of the emperor and the religious authority of the goddess.

While the Paphian sanctuary-type coins have long been used in discussions of Cypriote and Phoenician ar-

---

[4] Coins from Byblos, show a sanctuary of Aphrodite from an aerial perspective, making it clear that her baetyl sits inside an open courtyard. M. Price and B. Trell, Coins and their Cities, 1977, fig. 271, p. 150.

[5] For a good discussion on the term, "baetyl", see D. B. Thompson, Ptolemaic Oinochoai and Portraits in Faience, 1973, p. 62–69.

[6] H. Cain, Romische Marmorkandelaber,1985. On Severan coins, rings and a mirror they are sometimes changed into two additional baetyls. D. B. Thompson, Ptolemaic Oinochoai and Portraits in Faience, 1973, p. 67ff.

[7] G. Hill, Catalogue of the Greek Coins of Cyprus, 1904, repr. 1964, p. cxxix–cxxx. The first mention of the word "Paphian" Aphrodite in inscriptional material is in the Hellenistic age. T. Mitford, The Inscriptions of Kourion, 1971, p. 51, n. 2.

[8] There is clear evidence that the emperors chose many designs of coins in Rome. Examples include Julius Caesar, as pater patriae, (Dio Cassius, 44.4.4. and M. Crawford, Coinage of the Roman Republic, v. 1 and 2, 1974, p. 491, nos 19–20.), Augustus, with his selection of the capricorn symbol, (Suetonius, Aug. 94.12 and K. Kraft, Zum Capricorn auf den Munzen des Augustus, Jahrbuch fur Numismatik und Geldschichte 17, 1967, p. 17–27) , Nero, showing himself as Apollo Citharoedes, (Suetonius, Nero, 25.3 and H. Mattingly et al., Coins of the Roman Empire in the British Museum, 1923–1962, 1, nos. 234–238, 254–257, and 376–377) and Constantine, said to have selected his and his mother's portrait, with eyes gazing upwards, for the gold solidi. (Eusebius, Vita Const. 4.15. M. R. Alfoldi, Die constantinische Goldpragung, 1963, p. 128.)

[9] K. Harl, Civic Coins and Civic Politics in the Roman East , A.D. 180–275, 1987, p. 140, nt. 35.

[10] C. H. V. Sutherland, Roman Coins, 1974, p. 129–132 and p. 291, nt. 152. There are coins from Philippi with the inscription, "iussu aug" in P. Collart, Philippes: Ville de Macedonie depuis ses origines jusqu'a la fin de l'epoque romaine, p. 224–241 and C.H. V. Sutherland and C. M. Kraay, Catalogue of Coins of the Roman Empire in the Ashmolean Museum, I, Augustus, 1975, 1098 and from Patrae with the words, "indulgentia aug moneta" in M. Grant, From Imperium to Auctoritas: An Historical Study of Aes Coinage in the Roman Empire 49 B.C.–A.D. 14, 1946, p. 295, which may not be exceptions so much as including the obvious.

[11] S. Walker, The Image of Augustus, 1981, p. 19–27.

[12] This issue is still a matter of some controversy. S. R. F. Price, Rituals and Power: The Roman imperial cult in Asia Minor, 1984, p. 173–174 proposes the model of "choice by officials in Rome with a notional or even actual involvement of the emperor himself."

chitecture, with attempts at a reconstruction of the scanty archaeological remains of the Sanctuary of Aphrodite,[13] less attention has been paid to the actual meaning of the imagery as icons of imperial and provincial promotion and policy. Although the same gods, Zeus and Aphrodite, continued to be honored on Augustan coinage, two important visual changes from previous Hellenistic coins take place. First, the all-important portrait of the Roman Emperor replaced the Ptolemaic, deified ruler, following both Hellenistic and Republican Roman practice.[14] One earlier Hellenistic group of Paphian Greek coins showed Zeus and Aphrodite on opposite sides of the same coin, but in the early Empire, Augustus' portrait supplants one god. Under Augustus, two separate series are produced – one honoring Zeus and the other, Aphrodite, reflecting the importance of both deities on the island. This method is revised for the coins of Drusus where Aphrodite's sanctuary is combined on the same reverse with the sacrificing Zeus. It is, however, an inelegant solution, thrusting the composition off-balance and isn't attempted again. Most issues at Paphos thereafter continue to display two types separately, until Trajan, after which the Zeus type disappears altogether, under the Severans, in favor of Aphrodite.

A second innovation was in the imagery of Aphrodite. Instead of the former full-length or portrait head of the goddess on Hellenistic coins, she was represented by an unusual aniconic stone (baetyl) and architecture, a phenomenon rare before the Roman period.[15] This distinctive Paphian type proved very successful, since it lasted intact, with minor variations, for over two hundred years. It was a success based on its suitability as a recognizable sacred area for the island's inhabitants and, in addition, its expression of values through satisfying formal visual dichotomies. Regardless of Augustan coin imagery from other cities, the internal coherence of the Paphian coin's composition must have held strong meaning for the Cyprians. How exactly did the imperial representations of por-

trait and architecture function visually for the Augustan Empire as well as the local Paphian government? What did the imagery denote to the imperial representatives on the island, the Cyprians, the eastern Mediterranean tourist, and the Roman soldiers passing through the city? Why was the architectural image of the sanctuary of Aphrodite important to the Romans, when the anti-Classical facade and aniconic image appear so foreign to Roman religious conceptions?

Before examining the Augustan coins for their incipient imagery, it would be instructive to compare the changes in the later sanctuary types of Paphian coins from the Flavian and Severan dynasties. Bronzes from the Flavian period are exactly the same as the Augustan types, except for the portraits of the new ruler and his family. (Fig. 4) The reverse shows the same view of the sanctuary, except for a garland added between the gateposts and two stars flanking the baetyl, clearly attributing the image to Aphrodite. The sanctuary-type was indicative of the desired connection between the new dynasty and the revered "golden age" of Augustus, a method similar to the coinage program in Rome, where Trajan later closely imitated Augustan reverse types in an attempt to attach himself to the Julio-Claudian dynasty.[16]

A new series by Vespasian, however, was minted in addition to the bronze. Silver tetradrachms were coined in Paphos and displayed architectural details which were new. (Fig. 5) The semicircular courtyard disappears, and in place of the flanking candelabra are two new architectural wings, each consisting of three columns, the outer two connected by a low balustrade or fence. The new simplicity emphasizes the architectural tripartite form, indicative of remodeling, rather than symbols of the religion. This first appearance of columns could well represent what was in actual fact remodeling activity, since they appear in the year 76/77 A.D., the same year as the earthquake.[17] Silver coinage was most likely needed and produced for a large public program of construction or military project.

---

[13] See discussion in Appendix A.

[14] R. Hadley, *Deified Kingship and Propaganda Coinage in the early Hellenistic Age, 323–280 B.C.*, 1964.

[15] An unusual series of silver staters, dated to 520–425 B.C., tentatively assigned to Mallus in G. Hill, Catalogue of Greek coins of Lycaonia, Isauria, and Cilicia, 1904, pl. xvi.1–7, does show a baetyl flanked by obscure granulated objects, but it may be a freestanding pyramid.

[16] L. Laffranchi, Un Centenario Numismatico nell'Antichita, Rivista Italiana di Numismatica 24, 1911, p. 427–436. This policy was continued in Rome by the restoration types of both the obverse and reverse under Titus. H. Mattingly, Coins of Titus, Domitian, and Nerva, Numismatic Chronicle 20, 1920, p. 175–207.

Severan coins combined the Flavian silver type of sanctuary with an increased interest in religious symbol and detail. (Fig. 6) The side wings have one column supporting a roof. The paved and lattice-fenced semi-circular courtyard appears again. A star and crescent is over the central portion. Two birds sit upon the side roofs, two stars flank a baetyl, and candelabra sit within the side wings. In the court may be two or three circles, an irregular oval resembling a bird or fish, and a rectangular object below the baetyl. For the first time an Empress is shown on the obverse at Paphos, in addition to a separate series with the Emperor. The religious backgrounds and interests of Septimius and his wife Julia Domna are well attested. Julia Domna was the daughter of the Syrian high priest at Emesa of Elagabal, a Phoenician god equated with a sun-god, and honored as a black meteorite, like Aphrodite of Paphos.[18] Evidence of a strong Severan presence on the island can be seen in the amount of inscriptions and statuary.[19]

In returning to the question concerning the success of the basic Paphian sanctuary-type created in the Augustan period, it's obvious that the iconography of coins is forced by its dual-sided fields into specific visual dichotomies. I would argue that in the case of the Augustan Paphian bronzes, this requirement of coin iconography is taken advantage of, so that the meaning is amplified with particularly fortuitous choices of images for both their contrast and linked connotations. Three sets of oppositions are apparent. First, the portrait head of Augustus stands for imperial Rome versus the specific locality of Paphos as seen in the sanctuary. The former signifies the human ruler contrasted with the divine image of the baetyl. A second contrast is implied by the male ruler and the female goddess. The third and strongest visual opposition occurs between the organic portrait of Augustus and the non-organic, man-made structure of the sanctuary. These visual contrasts are tempered, though, by underlying links im-

plied by their juxtaposition, creating a single unified message.

The Augustan Paphian bronzes show the portrait head of Augustus on one side – a convention so long familiar and taken for granted, that it is prioritized by numismatists as the most important side, the obverse. He appears mortal, without the laurel wreath or radiate crown of later emperors. The emperor's portrait, as an emblem of Roman authority, promised prosperity and security to all outlying war-weary provinces. On a personal level, the emperor's image promised safety, even to slaves, who might flee to his public statue or imperial temple as a place of asylum.[20] The issue of asylum was particularly important to the Paphians, as an embassy was sent to Rome to plead their traditional right of asylum, which was then granted by Tiberius.[21] Why such a right was advantageous to the sanctuary may be seen in the custom of the payment of fines to imperial images,[22] and in the dignity and power such a privilege accorded to the priests.

The mortal ruler is contrasted to the immortal Paphian Aphrodite on the reverse side. The importance of Aphrodite (Venus) to the Julio-Claudian dynasty is clear, from the innumerable literary and artistic references to the goddess as ancestress to the family. With the birth of the second grandson of Augustus, in 17 B.C., the Julian family myth was again revived after a post-Actium concentration on Apollo as the antithesis of Mark Antony's Dionysus. The Roman world would be stabilized for the future if governed by the descendants of Augustus. Julia, for example, received honorary statues as Venus in 12 B.C. in the Greek East.[23] Venus was also crucial to the ruling family in her manifestation as Venus Victrix or Venus Armata,[24]

[17] See the discussions in G. Hill, A History of Cyprus, v. 1, 1940, p. 245 and E. Gardner, D. Hogarth, M. James, R. Smith, Excavations in Cyprus, 1887–88, Paphos, Leontari, Amargetti, Journal of Hellenic Studies, 9, 1888, p. 188–189 and 208, which are primarily based on the Chronicles of Eusebius.

[18] A. Birley, Septimius Severus, The African Emperor, 1972, p. 71.

[19] G. Hill, A History of Cyprus, 1949, p. 233.

[20] Stories of slaves fleeing to emperors' images are given in Philostratus, Vit. Apoll., I, 15; Pliny, Letter, x, 74; Ulpian in Digest, xxx, I, 19, I.

[21] Tact. Ann., III.62. Two inscribed pedestals, which were dedicated to Tiberius, were excavated by the British in 1888. E. Gardner, D. Hogarth, M. James, R. Smith, Excavations in Cyprus, 1887–88, Paphos, Leontari, Amargetti, Journal of Hellenic Studies, 9, 1888, p. 188.

[22] S. R. F. Price, Rituals and Power: The Roman Imperial Cult in Asia Minor, 1984, p. 193.

[23] P. Zanker, The Power of Images in the Age of Augustus, 1988, p. 193–221.

[24] J. Flemberg, Venus Armata, Sudien Zur Bewaffneten Aphrodite in Der Griechisch-Romischen Kunst, 1991.

as is seen especially in the numismatic evidence on a denarius from Rome of 31–29 B.C. Its obverse displays a portrait head of Augustus, with an inscription reading, CAESAR DIVI F, or Son of the Divine Julius Caesar. The reverse shows a standing Venus, armed with Mars' scepter, helmet and shield embellished with her eight pointed star.[25] The ironic connection of a sexually provocative Venus with the deadly weapons of Mars effectively reminded one of the fertile prosperity and military "virtus" of the family.

The Paphian engravers were careful that Aphrodite as goddess not outshine the emperor visually, and consequently they represented her as a baetyl, with much less visual weight than the former full-headed goddess on the Ptolemaic coins from Paphos.[26] A similar concept can be seen in the Augustus Prima Porta, where the hierarchic scale of the immortal Cupid is so much smaller than that of Augustus. Although the ruler is represented as mortal, without divine attributes, the meaning is tempered by one's awareness of his potential divinity, as a descendant of Venus and relation of the divine Caesar. He replaced a god or deified Hellenistic ruler on the Paphian coins. Ruler statues possessed, in addition to protective asylum, all the portentous power of an icon, apt to erupt in sweat[27] or other lifelike behavior worthy of a god. Like many cities throughout the Empire, Augustus' imperial cult was assigned to Paphos, which is referred to by inscriptions,[28]

and the city was renamed "Augusta" after being rebuilt in the 15 B.C. earthquake.[29]

Coins were not just a means of exchange, but were also religious votives.[30] Gifts of coins were brought to Aphrodite of Paphos by men who were sexually initiated there by priestesses.[31] As religious tokens, the value of coins would increase with appropriate imagery. Augustus, as mortal ruler, is elevated to divine status by Aphrodite, while the imperial respect and probable funding of the repairs on her sanctuary at Paphos enlarges her divine prestige, bringing the imperial and local realms of power into a symbiotic relationship.

Secondly, pairing Augustus with Aphrodite implies a contrast in gender. Augustus becomes the Mars to her Venus, in general Roman imagery. But the formerly anthropomorphized goddess of Greek Paphian coinage was in Roman times neutered into the aniconic stone or baetyl, usually explained as a sacred meteorite.[32] Although the baetyl, as an object of worship, certainly extended back to the Bronze Age in actual practice, the designers of the Paphian coins made a conscious archaizing decision to choose the image of a baetyl over a more conventional Greco-Roman full-length statue or portrait-head of Aphrodite. Rather than using the classicizing style of the 5th century B.C, typical of the Augustan iconography which signified a new world order in the city of Rome, the deliberate archaisms from prehistory in both architecture and baetyl of the Paphian sanctuary gave an ancient and therefore legitimate aura to current religious practices. By cap-

---

[25] P. Zanker, The Power of Images in the Age of Augustus, 1988, p. 73, doesn't differentiate between the six-pointed Sidus Caesaris, the 44 B.C. comet which Augustus co-opted as a symbol of Caesar's deification for the Ludi Victoriae Caesaris, and the eight-pointed star representing Near Eastern goddesses like Inanna-Ishtar-Aphrodite.

[26] Although in Rome, there are two series of carefully balanced coins, dated to pre-27 B.C., one with the head of Augustus with the full length portrait of Venus on the reverse and the other with the head of Venus and the full-length figure of Augustus on the reverse, S. Walker, The Image of Augustus, 1981, p. 26–27 and K. Kraft, Zur Munzpragung des Augustus, 1969, no such reversals occur in Cypriote coinage. Augustus always has visual prominence.

[27] Plutarch, Anthony, 60.2; and Suetonius, Vespasian, 5.6.

[28] G. Hill, A History of Cyprus, 1949, p. 234, note 1 and Inscriptiones Graecae ad Res Romanas pertinentes, 1906ff, III, 961 names Ceionia Callisto Attica the wife of a high-priest of the Augusti; IGRR III, 994 says that Salamis honors Hyllus son of Hyllus, who was the high-priest of Divus Augustus Caesar.

[29] Cassius Dio, LIV. 32.7 and LIV.25.

[30] Suetonius (Aug. 57) tells how the Romans threw gold coins into a lake in the Forum for the good health of Augustus for the New Years celebration.

[31] Clement of Alexandria, Exhort. II.13. Additional sources are Arnobius, Adv. Gentes, V and Julius Firmicus Maternus, De Errore Profanarum Religionum, c. 10.

[32] Both forms, baetyls and anthropomorphic statues, were used in the Paphian sanctuary. For the large black, polished stone of conical form found near the west boundary of the courtyard and now in the Nicosia Museum, see A. Westholm, Temples of Soli, 1936, p. 160. For the statue of Venus Armata from Nea Paphos, see J. Flemberg, Venus Armata, Sudien Zur Bewaffneten Aphrodite in Der Griechisch-Romischen Kunst, 1991. It was known that "representations (agalmation) of the goddess were sold at Paphos for visitors to take home", during the seventh or sixth century B. C. (Athenaeus, XV.676).

italizing on past, exotic forms of religious imagery and architecture, particularly when they came from the older Eastern tradition, the emperor and Rome could derive support from the provincial sanctuaries.

The deity in baetyl-form was worshipped widely throughout the ancient Near East.[33] Livy (xxix, 10, 4ff.), writes about such a stone, that had been brought to Rome. The Sibylline Books ordered that Cybele be transferred from Asia Minor to Rome in 204 B.C. Along with her image, even the original black meteorite in which she was worshipped was given to the Romans. The Phrygian Cybele would stabilize the new disorderly religious developments resulting from the Punic War,[34] promote the honor and standing of certain prominent families who traced their family line back to the Trojan warriors, and drive away foreign enemies.[35] Her temple, the Metroon, was built on the Palatine in 191 B.C., destroyed by fire and rebuilt in 110 B.C., again destroyed by fire and rebuilt by

Augustus.[36] The Metroon was next door to the Domus Augusti, so not only was the goddess a neighbor of Augustus, but she was connected specifically to the Julio-Claudian dynasty by means of Aeneas and Troy.[37] Baetyls were also used by Augustan designers as icons of Apollo, with a flat top similar to the Paphian stone.[38] So the baetyl-image had a familiar meaningful role to the Romans, as a stabilizing religious image.

The lack of feminine form in Aphrodite's imagery on the Paphian coins corresponds with the masculinization of Aphrodite in Roman Cyprus. The Paphian goddess does demonstrate qualities typical of any Aphrodite, those of regeneration and sexuality, since she was the consort of the resurrection god, Adonis.[39] An inscription from Amathus concerns the "hegetor" or priest of sacrifices for Aphrodite, who ordered the customary sacrifice to Aphrodite for the "fertility of the crops".[40] At Paphos, priests, rather than priestesses, controlled the sanctuary and divination,[41] only male victims were sacrificed[42] and gifts of coins were given to the goddess by men who were sexually initiated there. They in turn received salt and phalluses.

Paphia, in addition, had characteristics foreign to the Greek Homeric and Classical goddess; astral and martial

---

[33] Many later Roman provincial coins, particularly along the Pheonician coast, perhaps influenced by Paphos, also show baetyls. Examples include the Macrinus (217–218 A.D.) series from Byblos, showing a sanctuary or altar-court of Aphrodite. M. Price and B. Trell, Coins and their Cities, 1977, fig. 271, p. 150. There are remains of an 18th century B. C. sanctuary of obelisks at Byblos, which shows the antiquity of stone worship. Another baetyl, flat-capped like the one at Paphos, can be seen in the cart of Astarte on bronze coins from Sidon beginning in 116 A.D. G. Hill, Catalogue of Greek Coins of Phoenicia, repr. 1964, pl. xxiii.9. Twin "ambrosial rocks", according to the inscription, are part of the founding myth of Tyre, shown on coins from the reign of Gordian III. G. Hill, Catalogue of Greek Coins of Phoenicia, repr. 1964, pl. xxxiii.15. The Pergaean Artemis is shown in a pedimented shrine on Elagabalus' bronzes as a baetyl with two rows of dancers carved on it with crescent and star. G. Hill, Catalogue of Greek Coins of Lycia, Pamphylia, and Pisidia, repr. 1964, pl. xxiv.12. Twin baetyls representing the Dioscuri come from Sagalassus. G. Hill, Catalogue of Greek Coins of Lycia, Pamphylia, and Pisidia, repr. 1964, pl. xxviii.10 and 12. Mount Argaeus in Caesarea is represented like a mound on an altar flanked by two towers or standards on a long running series from Tiberius to Gordian III. G. Hill, Catalogue of Greek Coins of Galatia, Cappadocia, and Syria, repr. 1964, pl. xiii.1 and 2. From Emis come coins with the baetyl of Elagabalus in a pedimented temple. G. Hill, Catalogue of Greek Coins of Galatia, Cappadocia, and Syria, repr. 1964, pl.xxvii.12–14. Coins from Seleucia Pieria present the baetyl of Zeus Kasios (the mountain) inside a pedimented temple. G. Hill, Catalogue of Greek Coins of Galatia, Cappadocia, and Syria, repr. 1964, pl.xxx.iii.4, 7 and 8.

[34] Livy, xxv,1,6ff.

[35] M. Vermaseren, Cybele and Attis, the Myth and the Cult, 1977, p. 38ff. J. Perret, Les origines de la legende troyenne de Rome, 1942, p. 275. F. Bömer, Rom und Troja, 1951.

[36] Ovid, Fasti, iv, 347–348.

[37] P. Romanelli, 'Lo scavo al tempio della Magna Mater sul Palatino', Fondation Eugene Piot, Monuments et Memoires 46, 1962, p. 202–330. Maarten J. Vermaseren, Cybele and Attis, 1977, p. 41–43. In pl. 32 and 33, it's interesting that a relief of the facade of the Metroon on the Ara Pietatis from the time of Claudius doesn't depict the typical anthropomorphized cult statue on the pediment but only as an empty throne with Cybele's crown on top of it, which if the main image of Cybele was still a black meteorite, might be a more Greco-Roman way of referring to her than showing the actual stone.

[38] P. Zanker, The Power of Images in the Age of Augustus, 1988, p.89 and B. Kellum, Sculptural Programs and Propaganda in Augustan Rome: The Temple of Apollo on the Palatine, The Age of Augustus, R. Winkes, ed., 1985, p. 169–176.

[39] The founder priest of the Paphian Aphrodite's religion was said by Pindar (Pyth., II.15) to be Cinyras, the father of Adonis.

[40] C. Newton et al., The Collection of Ancient Greek Inscriptions in the British Museum, 1874–1916, IV, no. 975.

traits.[43] The Greeks had identified the Paphian goddess with Aphrodite in her manifestation as Urania, from the Near East.[44] She was recognized as being related to the Phoenician goddess, Astarte, who was similar to the Babylonian-Assyrian, Ishtar.[45] Another Cypriote city, Amathus, also worshipped Aphrodite-Ariadne, who was said to have a curious hermaphroditic image, since she was bearded, had male genitals and was dressed as a female.[46] Although the Cypriotes, no doubt, viewed the masculinized Aphrodite as an embodiment of totality, encompassing both male and female powers of creation, according to gender theorists, Roman authors tended to interpret hermaphrodites as infantile or diminished males.[47] Conceptualizing Aphrodite as a meteorite, then, bypasses such concerns, and emphasizes her prophetic power. Like her

Eastern equivalents, ultimately connected to the Sumerian goddess Inanna, she was also an incarnation of the planet Venus, and so was represented by the eight-pointed star symbol, a constant symbol in ancient Near Eastern art.[48] Her astral significance enabled her prophecy, so important to the political aspirations of the Romans.

The Paphian Aphrodite was also a war goddess. The Romans appeared to use Paphos as a rest and relaxation center, much like the cult of Venus in Eryx in Sicily,[49] for soldiers weary from war on the eastern front. Here, obvious oppositions of Augustus as warrior-male and Aphrodite as fertile-female are transcended by additional cross-currents of meaning. The formerly destructive warrior Augustus has redefined his image by 29 B.C. from that of victory into one emphasizing prosperity and growth.[50] The Paphian Aphrodite mediates between meanings of female rebirth and male concerns of dominance through war and politics. The meteoric stone may have characterized her martial and astral nature better for the Romans and Cypriotes than the usual sexualized, Hellenized models in nude anthropomorphic form.

A third contrast on the Paphian coin imagery exists between the large-scale head of Augustus on one side, which psychologically contains the most visual weight, and the relatively small-scale sanctuary facade and aniconic image of Aphrodite on the other. The profile of the emperor in hierarchic scale, of course, denoted Rome's official statement of power and centralized control,[51] and the reverse represented local religious powers, since the architecture is so clearly "foreign" in appearance. But here too the message of priority is not so clear-cut. Roman emperors were dependent on omens and divination from Venus, among others, to legitimize their rule. Titus, for

---

[41] The male priesthood at Paphos was extraordinarily powerful and wealthy. It held positions of such high rank that the last Ptolemaic king of Cyprus, when deposed by the Romans, was given the choice to become the priest of Paphos, as the next step down from king. He committed suicide instead, but that needn't necessarily refer to a "poor" offer. G. Hill, A History of Cyprus, 1949, 207–208.

[42] Tacitus, Histories, Book II, 3 and 4. Moses Hadas, ed. Alfred Church and W. Brodribb trans., Complete Works of Tacitus, 1942, p. 478–479.

> The victims are such as each worshiper has vowed, but males are selected; the surest prognostics are seen in the entrails of kids. It is forbidden to pour blood on the altar; the place of sacrifice is served only with prayers and pure flame, and though it stands in the open air, it is never wet with rain. The image of the goddess does not bear the human shape; it is a rounded mass rising like a cone from a broad base to a small circumference. The meaning of this is doubtful.

[43] P. Friedrich, The Meaning of Aphrodite, 1978, p. 80.

[44] Herodotus I.105 wrote that the Cypriote cult, as the Cyprians themselves admitted, was founded from the sanctuary at Ascalon in Phoenicia. Pausanias I.14 notes that the Assyrians first established the cult of Urania Aphrodite, and the Paphians of Cyprus and the Phoenicians at Ascalon in Palestine were the next.

[45] M. Marcovitch, From Ishtar to Aphrodite, Journal of Aesthetic Education, 30, summer 96, p. 43ff; and Z. Bahrani, The Hellenization of Ishtar; nudity, fetishism, and the production of cultural differentiation in ancient art, Oxford Art Journal, 19, 1996, p. 3ff.

[46] Macrobius, Sat. III, 8; Fragmenta Historicorum Graecorum, Muller, ed., 1878–1885, v. I, p. 386; Hesychius, s.v. Aphroditos; Catullus, 68, 51.

[47] G. Nugent, This Sex Which is Not One: De-Constructing Ovid's Hermaphrodite, Differences, 2, 1990, p. 163. and M. Olender, Aspects of Baubo: Ancient Texts and Contexts, Before Sexuality, The Construction of Erotic Experience in the Ancient Greek World, 1990, p. 105. This is different than the picture of wholeness presented by the androgynous forms in Plato's Symposium (189D–191D).

[48] An early, magnificent example is on the stele of Urnammu pictured in H. Frankfort, Art and Architecture of the Ancient Orient, 1954, p. 103.

[49] M. I. Finley, Ancient Sicily, 1979, p. 135.

[50] P. Zanker, The Power of Images in the Age of Augustus, 1988, p. 85 and 195ff. See a statue of Mars whose armor was carved with plants and cornucopiae, fig. 155b.

example, was immensely cheered, when consulting the priest of Paphos, to be told of his imminent reign.[52] Local sanctuaries were dependent on Rome for funding after disasters. The sanctuary was not just a representative of the goddess, but a gift and forceful reminder of the piety of the Emperor Augustus and Vespasian, who helped with earthquake repairs. The same relationship in Rome, between ruler and magistri of guild cults,[53] with Augustus bestowing gifts on a cult and the guilds returning the favor with an altar or statue with the epithet, Augusta, was extended to the provinces. The exchange formalizes imperial support and local loyalty. The imperial cult in the Greek provinces has been analyzed in terms of its importance as a communal, urban, local Greek phenomenon.[54] The imagery on provincial coinage promised values similar to the imperial cult: perpetual stability, local prestige, and a dynamic exchange with the central Roman authority.

The design of the Paphian sanctuary's architecture deserves emphasis. The two piers are a constant in the numismatic iconography on all Roman Paphian coin types. The gateway appears to have been a major indicator of the Paphian Aphrodite. One is reminded of the two sacred, bundled reed gateposts of Inanna that were distinctive markers of her and her temple's role as storehouse of grain, symbols of abundance. The motif of two pillars flanking an entrance is common throughout the ancient Near East, from the two columns in antis in a Trojan megaron, to the famous Biblical columns, Jachin and Boaz, that stood before the Phoenician influenced temple of Solomon at Jerusalem. Augustus was given the honor of planting twin laurel trees outside his residence in Rome.[55]

The roofing structure on the Paphian coins is also Eastern. The flat, crenelated roof of the second type of coinage at Paphos of Drusus is identical to the coins from Chalcis in Phoenicia, which have a two-columned structure enclosing a baetyl, from the first century A.D. Assyrian seals show the antiquity of the Paphian sanctuary's architectural features. A Neo-Assyrian (1000–612 B.C.) sealstone displays two piers, connected by a balustrade and a crenelated roof enclosing a column, represented by the same short-hand elements as on the Paphian coins.[56] Middle Kingdom Assyrian sealstones from c. 2000 B.C. show the typical Assyrian gateway, two piers elongated to fit on a small surface, framing an altar, on which a deity image stands (probably the dog of the healing goddess, Gula) under an eight-pointed star.[57] In spite of the vast difference in date between the Assyrian seal and the Paphian coins, the connections in iconography are likely, given the origin of the Aphrodite religion in the Babylonian-Assyrian goddess Ishtar.

The formal composition of the sanctuary as seen on the Augustan coin has long been recognized as an Augustan feature, whether called "tripartite",[58] an "heraldic composition",[59] or the more biological term, "bilateral symmetry". Although difficult to correlate to actual architecture, the symmetrical composition, consisting of one

[51] E. H. Swift, Imagines in imperial portraiture, American Journal of Archaeology, 27, 1923, p. 286ff.; M. Stuart, How Were Imperial Portraits Distributed Throughout the Roman Empire?, American Journal of Archaeology, 43, 1939, p. 600–617; S. R. F. Price, Rituals and Power: The Roman imperial cult in Asia Minor, 1984, p. 173ff.; P. Zanker, Studien zu den Augustus-Portrats. I: Der Actium-Typus, 1973; and P. Zanker and K. Vierneisel, Die Bildnisse des Augustus, 1979.

[52] Tacitus, Histories, Book II, 4. Moses Hadas, ed. Alfred Church and W. Brodribb, trans., Complete Works of Tacitus, 1942, p. 478–479.

> Titus, after surveying the treasures, the royal presents, and the other objects which the antiquarian tendencies of the Greek arbitrarily connect with some uncertain past, first consulted the oracle about his voyage. Receiving an answer that the way was open and the sea propitious, he then, after sacrificing a number of victims, asked some questions in ambiguous phrase concerning himself. Sostratus (that was the name of the priest) seeing that the entrails presented an uniformly favorable appearance, and that the goddess signified her favor to some great enterprise, returned at the moment a brief and ordinary answer, but afterwards soliciting a private interview, disclosed the future. His spirits raised, Titus rejoined his father…

[53] P. Zanker, The Power of Images in the Age of Augustus, 1988, p.134.

[54] S. R. F. Price, Rituals and Power: The Roman imperial cult in Asia Minor, 1984, chap. 3.

[55] P. Zanker, The Power of Images in the Age of Augustus, 1988, p.93.

[56] E. Porada, Mesopotamian Art in Cylinder Seals of the Pierpont Morgan Library, 1947, p. 60–61, no. 79.

[57] H. Frankfort, The Art and Architecture of the Ancient Orient, Baltimore, 1956, fig. 24.B, p. 68.

tall element flanked by two shorter mirrored objects, had a long and revered history in the Ancient Near East. So prevalent as to be often ignored in modern scholarship, this composition once had a very specific meaning. Mesopotamian examples show a central divine figure (male or female), with shorter, mirrored animals facing towards or away from the center. The inclusion of vines or flowing water makes the allusion to agricultural and human prosperity clear. The Assyrians continue with this composition in the form of a central tree flanked by genii or kings. Its rarity before the New Kingdom in Egypt,[60] except perhaps in the architecture of the hypostyle hall (which represents the papyrus of the fertile Delta and abundant life), witnesses its probable transmission as a compositional type, rather than indigenous. In Rome, the age of Augustus sees a renewed interest in bi-lateral compositions,[61] and the central element continues to carry meanings of procreation and prosperity.

When fully considered then, the inclusiveness in meaning of the Paphian sanctuary-type determined its success. Mortal and divine spheres are brought together to elevate and legitimize the Roman ruler and, at the same time, stress the validity of Paphos as the birthplace of the ancestress of that ruler. Male and female elements are combined to emphasize the male roles of war and political life-important on imperial and local levels. Biological and architectural images reinforce one another, to bring an archaic, exotic, and therefore authentic meaning to the religion of Aphrodite.

---

[58] M. Price and B. Trell, Coins and their Cities, 1977, p. 147ff. The authors assume that the three parts of architecture on the Paphian coins are to be equated with three cellas directly behind it. The architectural remains at Paphos and the traditions of other baetyls and courtyards make such a premise unlikely.

[59] P. Zanker, The Power of Images in the Age of Augustus, 1988, p. 97. This is a term more reminiscent of its function on a medieval coat of arms than indicative of its original purpose in the Ancient Near East.

[60] The tomb of Memna has a wonderful New Kingdom example. G. Robins, Women in Ancient Egypt, 1993, p. 187–189.

[61] For a well-known example, see the terracotta plaque of Apollos' phallic baetyl and two maidens from the sanctuary of Apollo on the Palatine. B. Kellum, Sculptural Programs and Propaganda in Augustan Rome: The Temple of Apollo on the Palatine, The Age of Augustus, R. Winkes, ed., 1985, p. 169–176.

## Appendix A

Early interpretations of the Paphian sanctuary were simply descriptions of what the Severan coin type looked like. T. Donaldson, Architectura Numismatica, 1859, repr. 1966; M. Ohnefalsch-Richter, Kypros, the Bible, and Homer, 1893. F. Munter, Der Tempel der Himmlischen Gottin zu Paphos, 1924; C. G. Lanz, Die Gottin von Paphos, 1924; C. Blinkenberg, Le sanctuaire de Paphos, 1924.

After the site at Paphos was first excavated by the British in 1888, there was an extensive discussion in E. Gardner, D. Hogarth, M. James, R. Smith, Excavations in Cyprus, 1887–88, Paphos, Leontari, Amargetti, Journal of Hellenic Studies 9, 1888, p. 147–271, concerning the relation of the architectural remains to the coin representations, but the elevation on the coins didn't correspond to one particular architectural area. The site consists of a southern wing dated to the Bronze Age and a northern section of Roman date. V. Karageorghis, Chronique des Fouilles a Chypre en 1975, BCH 100, 1976, p. 886. The northern section has a central court bordered by two stoas and several rooms. Two monumental entrances, twenty feet wide, on the east and south sides, lead to a large walled courtyard, with altars, surrounded by small, irregular rooms.

A courtyard-sanctuary rather than a temple is paralleled by all other non-Hellenized Cypriote sanctuaries, like those at Idalion, Voni, Frangissa, Achna, (M. Ohnefalsch-Richter, Ancient Places of Worship in Kypros, 1891, pl. X; M. Ohnefalsch-Richter, Cypros, the Bible and Homer, 1893, pl. X), the archaic sanctuary of Apollo at Kourion, (R. Scranton, Sanctuary of Apollo at Kourion, Transactions of the American Philosophical Society, 1967, p. 575) and the Sanctuary of Athena at Vouni (A. Westholm, Temples of Soli, Stockholm, 1936, 157, fig. 74). A final additional example is at Soli, where in two sanctuaries, B (of Aphrodite) and D (of Isis), the Hellenistic structures were walled enclosures with rooms at the rear (A. Westholm, Temples of Soli, 1936, p.94).

E. Gardner, Excavations in Cyprus, 1887–88, Paphos, Leontari, Amargetti, Journal of Hellenic Studies, 9, 1888, p. 212, and A. Westholm, The Paphian sanctuary of Aphrodite, Acta Archaeologica, 1933, p, 200, considered the frontal court at Paphos to be rectangular, represented as circular on the coins to conform to the round frame. Price and Trell, Coins and their Cities, 1977, fig. 270, however, show a 7th century B.C. model of a shrine from Lemnos, which has a semi-circular forecourt. Also, the court is not only pictured on round coins, but also a rectangular gold box and an elongated gem, where the semi-circle didn't conform to the field. There are a group of remains in Cyprus which have been classified as altars and are large, paved, semi-circular platforms. Examples are Altar 146 in Sanctuary B at Soli, the altar outside the courtyard of the sanctuary of Athena at Vouni, and an altar, archaic in date, in the precinct of the sanctuary of Apollo at Kourion. So a semi-circular forecourt poses little problem.

Although the east entrance, with its two large pier foundations, corresponds best with the coin representations, and a huge black, polished stone of conical form, now in the Nicosia Museum, was found near the west boundary of the courtyard, A. Westholm, Sanctuaries of Soli, 1936, p.160, since so little of the sanctuary has been excavated, most later commentators see little relation between the coin representation and the actual architecture.

**Fig. 1A and B.** ANS 1944.100.75838, Bronze Ptolemaic coin, a. Obv. Head of Aphrodite, facing right, b. Rev. Eagle, left. Photo courtesy of the American Numismatic Society.

**Fig. 2A and B.** ANS 1952.142.257, Bronze Augustan coin, a. Obv. Head of Augustus, facing right, b. Rev. Sanctuary of Aphrodite. Photo courtesy of the American Numismatic Society.

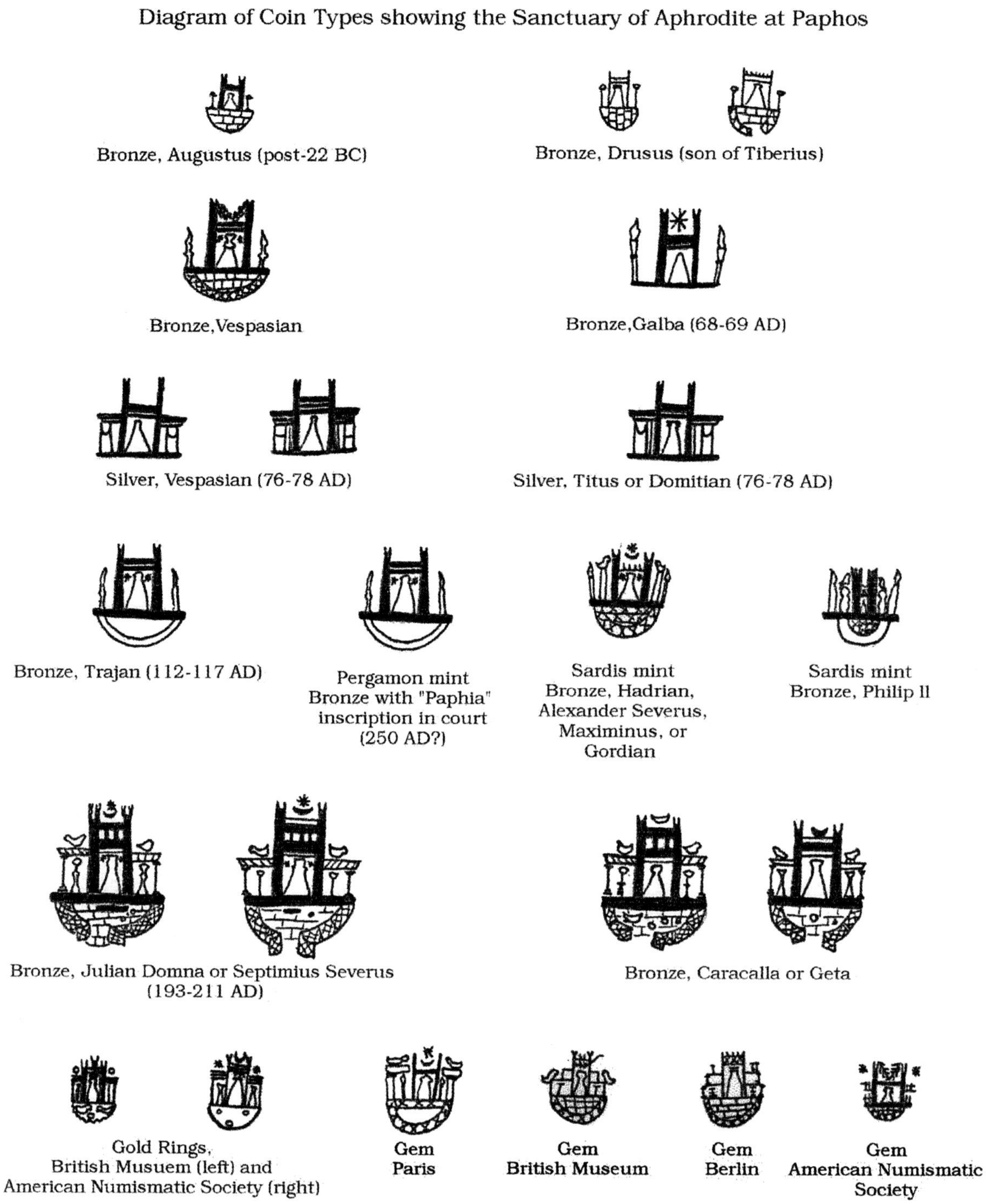

## Diagram of Coin Types showing the Sanctuary of Aphrodite at Paphos

Bronze, Augustus (post-22 BC)

Bronze, Drusus (son of Tiberius)

Bronze, Vespasian

Bronze, Galba (68-69 AD)

Silver, Vespasian (76-78 AD)

Silver, Titus or Domitian (76-78 AD)

Bronze, Trajan (112-117 AD)

Pergamon mint
Bronze with "Paphia"
inscription in court
(250 AD?)

Sardis mint
Bronze, Hadrian,
Alexander Severus,
Maximinus, or
Gordian

Sardis mint
Bronze, Philip II

Bronze, Julian Domna or Septimius Severus
(193-211 AD)

Bronze, Caracalla or Geta

Gold Rings,
British Musuem (left) and
American Numismatic Society (right)

Gem
Paris

Gem
British Museum

Gem
Berlin

Gem
American Numismatic
Society

**Fig. 3.** Diagram of the major types of the Sanctuary of Aphrodite of Paphos on coins and gems. (Drawn by the author.)

**Fig. 4A and B.** ANS 1944.100.62176, Bronze Vespasianic coin, a. Obv. Head of Vespasian, facing right, b. Rev. Sanctuary of Aphrodite. Photo courtesy of the American Numismatic Society.

**Fig. 5A and B.** ANS 1944.100.57136, Silver Vespasianic tetradrachm, a. Obv. Head of Vespasian, facing left, b. Rev. Sanctuary of Aphrodite. Photo courtesy of the American Numismatic Society.

**Fig. 6A and B.** ANS 1944.100.62199, Bronze Severan coin, a. Obv. Head of Julia Domna, facing right, b. Rev. Sanctuary of Aphrodite. Photo courtesy of the American Numismatic Society.

# The Authors

Susan Heuck Allen is Lecturer in Archaeology at Smith College and Visiting Scholar in Classics at Brown University, 98 Transit Street, Providence, Rhode Island, 02906.

Joseph J. Basile is Professor in the Department of Art History, Maryland Institute, College of Art, 1300 Mt. Royal Avenue, Baltimore, Maryland, 21217.

Catheryn Leda Cheal is an Instructor in the Art Department at California State University Northridge, Northridge, California, 91330.

Derek B. Counts took his PhD. in Old World Archaeology and Art at Brown University in 1998. Address: 317 Lamartine Street, Apt. 1, Jamaica Plain, Massachusetts, 02130.

Owen Doonan is a Dyson Postdoctoral Fellow at the University of Pennsylvania, Museum of Archaeology and Anthropology, 33rd and Spruce Streets, Philadelphia, Pennsylvania 19104-6324.

Susan S. Lukesh is Associate Provost and Interim Dean of Libraries, Hofstra University, 128 Hofstra, Hempstead, New York, 11550-1090.

Brian E. McConnell is an External Collaborator of the Superintendency of Cultural Property for the Province of Catania and Visiting Scholar of the Center for Old World Archaeology and Art at Brown University, Viale A. De Gasperi 241, Catania, CT 95127, Italy.

Frances Van Keuren is Professor in the Graduate Faculty, Lamar Dodd School of Art, University of Georgia, Athens, Georgia 30602-4102.

Printed by E. A. Johnson Co.